EDITING

ACADEMIC

TEXTS advanced verb form

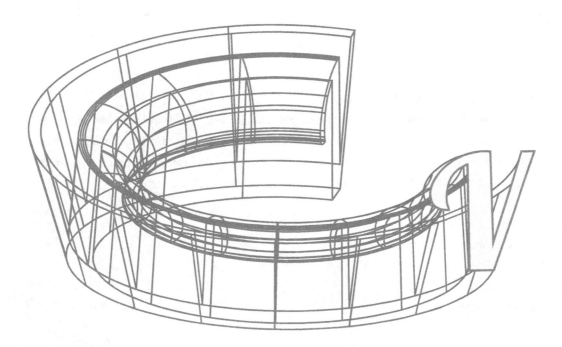

CC Undertree

GramEd SERIES

Cover Designer: Hossro Khorsand
Website: http://hossro.graphics

coleman's
classroom

Request for special permission should be addressed to:
Coleman's Classroom
Attn. CC Undertree
11138 Del Amo Blvd. STE 174
Lakewood, CA 90715

Website: www.ccundertree.com
E-mail: ccundertree@gmail.com

ISBN-10: 1717326439
ISBN-13: 9781717326430

ACADEMIC VOCABULARY

Because vocabulary development is a never-ending process for college students, especially non-native English speakers, this book, in addition to being a grammar editing book, indicates academic vocabulary words throughout the text with either an asterisk * for Academic Word List (AWL) or a star ✧ for bonus advanced vocabulary. An itemized* list of all the vocabulary can be found in Appendix H.

Professor Undertree's tone makes me feel as we are having a conversation, and the tips are very clear and easy to follow. This book is easy for ESL students to study!
~ Amanda Peng, ESL Student

This book aroused my interest and curiosity as soon I opened it because I felt as if I were having a face-to-face dialogue with Professor Undetree to learn the editing strategies and verb forms. This book is clearly positioned to improve academic writing through self-editing!
~ Liping Li, ESL Student

Writing is a good tool for those who know how to manage it. The grammar sections to review my tenses and the paragraph texts for editing practice were so helpful!
~ Ximena Barco, ESL Student

I really love the examples! I read many grammar books, but the examples in Professor Undertree's book were some of the most useful!
~ Mania Takmilnejad, ESL Student

The Overview Verb Pattern Charts really helped my understanding. This is such a helpful book. I'd like to read others!
~Tiffany Thy To, ESL Student

I liked the Isolation Strategy the most! These edits were perfect practice, and I could learn from my grammar mistakes.
~Maryam Khazaei, ESL Student

Professor Undertree's passion in teaching from the heart helped me learn fully. Following the Editing Strategies made a great change in my writing. I also really benefitted from the Bonus Vocabulary! It is a unique idea I haven't seen in other books.
~Tina Gharai, ESL Student

I really loved this book! I especially liked the Study Tips and Editing Strategies because they teach how to self-correct and write carefully. This book is such a useful resource for ESL students who want to be better writers!
~ Marwa Elmossallamy, Supplemental Instructor

As a teacher and editor myself, I can't overstate the importance of learning effective editing strategies, and this book empowers students to do exactly that.
~ Eric de Roulet, English Tutor and Graduate Student

I love how this book provides so many learning resources! I can use the model paragraphs for writing, the vocabulary lists for reading, the grammar charts for reviewing, and the practice paragraphs for editing! This is a great all-in-one resource for my classes!
~ Randi Perlman, ESL Instructor

TABLE OF CONTENTS

TABLE OF CONTENTS

ACKNOWLEDGMENTS

A grassroots✧ book like this would not have been possible without those who encouraged me to push the boundaries of the possible and aided me throughout the process. As such it is vital to acknowledge the support of the countless individuals who contributed to the content herein.

I must thank my amazing ESL students who dedicated their time, energy, and ideas to these materials.

I want to thank my 2016 summer reader panel*, Maryam Khazaei, Gabriela Rocha, Amanda Peng and Tiffany Thy Tho. Your feedback in the initial stages of the book offered me direction and encouragement. It took longer than anticipated to get it done, but as promised, here it is!

Thank you to my Irvine Valley College ESL classes throughout 2016- 2017 who practiced completing so many of the edits in class and graciously forgave the many mistakes they discovered; your enthusiasm for learning and editing* more effectively spurred✧ me forward through moments of disappointment and exhaustion.

Thank you to my 2017 summer reader panel, Mania Takmilnejad, Sohelia Rashedi, Ximena Barco, Amanda Peng, Tina Gharai, Liping Ni, and Marwa El-Mossallamy, I am grateful for your insight and suggestions! Special thanks to Amanda Peng for reading two summers in a row!

Also to Tina Gharai, from Dreamseed Graphics Design, who created the arrow for Chart 5 and 6, thank you for all the detailed advice you gave me on the charts and formatting!

Many thanks to you, Liping Ni, for your suggestion to add the quotes so that it feels more like our class website and for your ideas about having fun while editing. Appendices G and I were inspired by you! And to you Amin Ahrari for introducing me to the Shiraz poets and helping me find the perfect quote from Hafez; from one language lover to another, you are the best!

Mahnoosh Rahimi, thank you for the title feedback and all the other detailed suggestion you gave me.

Lucas Nguyen (soon to be Dr. Nguyen!), you inspire me to reach for the impossible every day. My tiny part in your success makes me think that I can make a difference in other students' lives too!

Though it is impossible to individually name all the countless classroom and LAC students who have emboldened✧ me to share my lessons with others, know that you have made teaching writing, grammar, and language such a pleasure! I wouldn't be doing this but for you! Thank you all!

Finally, for all students who despair of ever mastering this English language, I give you my Graphic Artist Hossro Khorsand. Once, like you, he was a student in my community college writing class. Though he didn't specifically love language or writing or grammar, he understood the need for excellence to pursue his dreams. Now, he is finishing up his BFA and beginning his career in artistic design. As the primary designer of so many important elements of this book, specifically the cover, graphics, and many of the text layouts, he was able to take my medium of ideas and words and translate it into his medium of visual representation. Any errors with these elements are completely mine. I couldn't be more proud of his work and accomplishments. His achievements prove that diligent hard work can lead to success, for him, for me, and for each one of you!

Educators in the USA often have a thankless job regarding monetary recompense✧ or societal respect. Nonetheless, where it ultimately matters in the halls of history and the lives of those they touch, their influence, insight, and effort are priceless. I would not be where I am today without the help and camaraderie✧ I have received from my own professors and from my academic colleagues*.

While it is impossible to individually acknowledge every educator who shaped me and ultimately this book, I do want to recognize some of my particularly influential instructors. Dr. Wheeler, could you have imagined that paragraphs I wrote for you would end up in a grammar editing book? Thank you for pushing me then toward writing excellence. Professor Lipton, you always insisted that I didn't need an MFA in writing to pursue my goals. Once again, sir, you were right. Dr. Wallech, the questions you asked me when I sought your advice enabled me to find my own answers. Professor Potter, had you not believed in me so long ago, this book would not be here today. Every student I will ever help in the future owes a debt of gratitude to you all.

My friend and fellow ESL instructor Randi Perlman cheered me on through every single chapter even piloting some of the materials in her own class; this book would have been so much less without your unflagging* support. I don't have the words to express how this means to me.

Kim Rainstar has seen me through three books now. We've come a long way since CSULB, haven't we? Thank you, Kim, for dreaming such galvanizing* dreams and provoking me to do the same.

Many other fellow faculty members had a hand or voice one way or another in this final* project, and I appreciate* all of you, specifically Susan Akhavan, Vanessa Russell, Nathan Cayanan, Peyman Pakshir, Susan Fesler, Heather Stern, Rebecca Beck, Marwa Elmossallamy, Mark Makino, and Eric de Roulet.

Special thanks to Eric de Roulet for your amazing editing skills; your insight into the infinitesimal* linguistic details was so marvelous! Your clever comments actually made me laugh out loud at some of my mistakes! This admirable skill of taking the sting out of an error will be a great asset to you in the classroom. You're the best!

Finally, though not educators themselves, my family has been a huge part of this book. No one has listened to more of my teaching stories and endless writing angst* than they. I want to thank Sam and Roger Coleman for listening despite having little specific interest in academic editing just because you care about me.

Thank you to the Pirate for applying your own knowledge of running a ship to my experiences, which helped me see solutions I would have missed.

Thank you to the Hunter, whose continuous support and witty wisecracks* throughout my life have helped me see that no knowledge or experience is ever wasted.

I must once again honor those that have passed out of my life for now, my beloved mother, my Grandma and Grandpa Talbot, and my Grandma Smith. I was blessed to have them in my life, and I miss them every day. Their absence makes me strive daily to be the best I can since tomorrow may never come.

Most significantly, none of my writing or work for Coleman's Classroom would be possible without the anchor of my life and support for all I do, Mr. C. Thank you for always being there from the beginning and staying until the last chapter will be written.

2018 Update: Special thanks to my Fall 2017 and Spring 2018 students at Irvine Valley College for piloting the first version of the book. Your insight and feedback was invaluable for me for this and future projects! I am especially grateful to Shayan Gheidari, Tania Acosta, Cindy Dang, Jeongae Kim, Shohreh Malekzadeh, Kathy Rahimi, Karen Vargas, Kay El Moussaoui, Justin Woo, and Yeong Je Lee for your detailed feedback on specific book issues. Finally, I couldn't possibly accomplish all I do without the unfailing support of my small dedicated tribe who inspire me every day -- you know who you are; these resources would not exist without you. As I tell my students, we bring to our writing all that we are; simply put, I would not be me without you, and I am so appreciative of the support that has brought me to this point so that I can bring these writing resources to others.

Only those who dare to fail greatly

can ever achieve greatly.

~Robert Kennedy

CHAPTER 1

INTRODUCTION

Welcome

Using This Book

Why Verb Form?

One today is worth two tomorrows;

never leave for tomorrow

what you can do today.

~Benjamin Franklin

Welcome to Coleman's Classroom!!

My name is CC Undertree, Professor Undertree to my students, and I am a composition and language instructor* in Southern California. I have been facilitating college students' improvement in their writing abilities since 1999. Having taught all levels of college writing from basic language development to critical thinking across the curriculum, I have seen most every kind of writing prompt and problem in college level composition. I have observed countless students struggle with college-level writing dilemmas, which encompass* not just the writing itself, but all the affiliated required* skills of grammar usage, vocabulary sufficiency, critical thinking, reading ability and more.

Through these experiences, I have learned that there is no one strategy or technique* that will lead to writing improvement; the process is multifaceted* and complex*. Nevertheless, an activity that can be greatly beneficial to good writing is the mastery of personal editing strategies, which promote polished academic writing. Such mastery requires specific and extensive practice to develop the desired skills. This book has been written to target* just that kind of editing proficiency.

Knowing what you want is the first step to getting it.
~Louise Hart

There are many, many books, online exercises, and language classes available* for students today; some focus* on real-life writing, and others on scholastic* academic writing. In my experience, my students are generally seeking one source to meet all their goals of increased correct grammar, outstanding vocabulary usage, and excellent composition skills. It should also be satisfactorily engaging, culturally informative, suitably motivating, and reasonably priced! Whew! That's a lot to ask from just one book!

Nonetheless, a great thing about writing one's own book is that the author has the power to include all the things she wishes were in other books, and I have done so here by striving* to fulfill as many desired aspects as possible with the overall aim of helping you become secure* in the knowledge that your grammar in your writing is the best that it can possibly be through a bit of grammar review and repeated editing practice.

The primary* goal herein* is to reinforce* prior* grammar study while providing some straightforward* and limited strategies that will enable* writers to master effective editing through the extensive and repetitious application of the concepts*. These methods* have proven successful in not only my own personal writing but also in my advanced ESL students' writing.

Live as if you were to die tomorrow.
Learn as if you were to live forever.
~Mahatma Gandhi

Additionally, in a secondary goal to model quality academic writing, I have incorporated* common kinds of structures* and topics in the practice editing paragraphs. Employing college-level paragraphs for the grammar and editing practice encourages an authentic writing context* to make the most of students' time and effort in learning. You may notice a difference in font and paragraphing in the Practice Edits; this is a deliberate attempt to replicate as much as possible the look and feel of student academic collegiate writing.

To meet a third goal of facilitating reading development, critical academic vocabulary has been indicated throughout the book with a small asterisk, like so* to the immediate right of specific words from the Academic Word List (AWL) vocabulary. The AWL is a generally accepted group of words necessitated in college level writing. You have probably already noted these * on this page. You might have also noticed another symbol like this ❖ next to words here and there. This symbol will occasionally be used to indicate bonus vocabulary that is not part of the AWL but still should be used in your writing.

Other goals of engaging and informing students are more challenging to meet through grammar instruction. Even so, I have attempted to satisfy these demands through the paragraph content, which subtly highlights academic topics and culturally relevant* information, and through the usage of example boxes, study tips, and emphasized text. To motivate, I apply the same techniques used in my face-to-face classes including a personal tone and motivating expressions of others much more accomplished than I. And for price... reasonably priced is always tough.

How does one put a price on knowledge? On empowerment? On better writing? On language mastery? It is not possible to do so, yet a price must be set regardless. While this book is not free, I have tried to keep the cost down as much as possible, and I do have free resources available for you at Coleman's Classroom for your language development. I would hope that the cost of educational resources never keeps you from increasing your language skills.

Providing a comprehensive* grammar primer* is beyond the scope* of this book as is exhaustive writing instruction. If you are looking for a resource* with in-depth grammar lessons or writing instruction, you will not find it here! The level of the practice edits in this book assumes* you have a basic solid foundation in English grammar, vocabulary, and writing. The editing exercises in *Editing Academic Texts: Advanced Verb Form* are designed* to accompany, not replace, educator-lead grammar or writing instruction. The purpose of these exercises is to provide students with targeted grammatical editing using academic paragraphs* to enable the improvement of specific language aspects*, specifically English verb form.

*The beautiful thing about learning
is that nobody can take it away from you.*
~B.B. King

Using this Book

Before we can dive into the awesomeness of editing, it is a good idea to understand the bigger writing picture. What is required in academic writing? Why do grammar errors even occur in the first place? Why, no matter how much time and effort you put into your study, do you keep making the same grammar mistakes over and over again in your papers? How can you overcome these challenges? Chapter 2's sections on Understanding Writing Processes and Understanding Grammar Errors will enable you to answer these questions with an explanation of the cyclical nature of writing and the three causes of grammar errors with solutions for each.

Also, Chapter 2 will introduce some new editing strategies; why, however, should you need them at all? As a student writer, you already have some editing strategies, but are these strategies the best ones to use? Ask yourself if the editing strategies you've been using have been effective. Are your grades in writing classes what you hope they will be? Are you pleased with your final product? Only you can know what you have done successfully thus far and where your weaknesses lie.

If you are like so many of my students, I would hazard to guess that your editing strategies are less than ideal. The one I see the most from students is simply reading and rereading and then rereading the paper for errors*. Despite this extreme reading effort, the grammar errors are unfortunately often missed by students, a circumstance which creates frustration and dissatisfaction. Learning to recognize grammar mistakes is an area* in which most people need instruction and practice, so I highly advise you to spend some time learning the new strategies before beginning the reviews and practice.

The Editing Strategy Instruction provides specific* effective techniques for editing written text*. The first, Focus Practice, is based on my belief of the benefit* of tightly focusing on specific aspects of writing to master them. The second, Isolate Errors, has been greatly beneficial for my students. If you can learn only one of the strategies, I suggest Isolate Errors be the one. The Read Aloud Strategy may be one of the most difficult to cultivate. Next, the Take Breaks strategy* requires good time management skills for its productive application. Finally, the Have Fun strategy is important for long-term editing success.

All these techniques have been proven in my own writing as well as in my students'. Since you have decided to improve your grammar editing methods, why don't you take the time to incorporate all the new strategies into your personal editing system? The more editing strategies you can effectively use, the better your academic writing will be.

Following the Editing Strategies Instruction, the grammar review and practice chapters briefly address the kind of common verb form errors I see in my students' college writing. If you want to concentrate on your own error patterns, then you can jump right to that review and practice, or if you want a more extensive review and practice, you can go through the topics one by one. The review begins with an irregular verb form mini-lesson in Chapter 3; this chapter provides an accompanying review list of all the irregular verbs used in this book in Chapter 10: Appendix D.

Education is the passport to the future,
for tomorrow belongs to those who prepare for it today.
~Malcolm X

Chapter 4 offers a quick look at the verbal forms of the gerund, simple participle* adjective and phrasal participle adjective forms. Next, in Chapter 5, the important subject-verb agreement review covers some particular problem areas with gerunds, indefinite* pronouns, collective nouns, relative pronouns, and irregular adverbs. Perhaps the most complicated of them all is Chapter 6 with its brief* survey*, for both active and passive voice, of the verb tense pattern forms and the modal forms as well. Finally, Chapter 7 reviews incorrect verb pattern shifting*. Each of these chapters provides five Practice Edits; the number of errors for only the first three is indicated* in the instructions to aid* you in your initial practice.

After these focused grammar reviews, Chapter 8: Combined Editing Practice, provides twenty-eight more Practice Edits and coalesces* all the errors to provide an authentic editing practice. In real writing, errors are not nicely isolated* for our editing convenience. Real editing is messy because grammar errors are messy.

Moreover, for the majority of these Practice Edits, the number of errors will not be indicated. For focused practice, it is crucial* to practice in as genuine circumstances* as possible. When you edit your own work, you will not know how many errors you may have, so the most beneficial practice will occur when the exact number of errors in these exercises is unrevealed in advance. This is the same reason that the final two Practice Edits in each review chapter do not indicate the error count. Often times, students create* errors when there were none when looking for a specific number of errors! Therefore, it is better in the long run for your editing development to have an unknown number of errors in the exercises.

Champions keep playing until they get it right.
~Billy Jean King

It is also necessary to check your results through your practice editing to verify your understanding and progress. Thus, the back page of each Practice Edit will provide some Suggested Answers, with the errors corrected and indicated* by number and bold text. The Answers Explained section will provide a brief explanation for each correction. It may be possible to have more than one answer for some of the errors, but the given Suggested Answers will be the most common. With each suggested answer in Chapter 8, the related chapter designation will be given so you can easily go back and review again as needed.

The book is wrapped up with Chapter 9: Final Notes from my classroom. As in my own classes, I always like to conclude* a lesson with a summary* of what was learned, it's relevance to a larger topic, and a bit of future encouragement. You'll find that information in Chapter 9.

Chapter 10: Appendices provides important information and reference materials. The first five Appendices conveniently compile all important references for the book's abbreviations and formulas (Appendix A), grammar charts and example boxes (Appendix B and C), irregular verbs (Appendix D), and Works Cited* (Appendix E). Then, Appendix F addresses the second goal of the book, model writing with information on paragraph types and content with an added bonus quote index in Appendix G that also has prompts for your own writing practice. Appendix H covers the third goal of academic vocabulary development with the AWL and bonus vocabulary with page numbers of accentuated* vocabulary throughout the book. Finally, Appendix I provides some suggestions for having fun with editing.

O someone should start laughing!
Someone should start widely Laughing Now!
~Hafez

You may wish to deeply explore some of the Appendices resources or ignore them entirely. You may decide to use them at the beginning of your study, by reviewing in advance the academic vocabulary or model writing information, or you might decide to look up the vocabulary as you encounter* the asterisks in your reading. Again, there is no correct sequence in using these materials; instead, incorporate them into your study in ways that work best for you!

Study Tip

This book has a high level of language since it is an Advanced ESL guide. I suggest you divide your efforts into manageable components. Don't compound the difficulty by doing too much at the same time. Focus on the grammar or focus on the vocabulary or focus on the writing samples. Try and expand one skill at a time, so you don't overwhelm yourself with widespread panic!

Nothing great was ever achieved without enthusiasm.
~Ralph Waldo Emerson

Why Verb Form?

It is impossible to master all aspects of academic writing at once; to effectively master high level writing in a language, one must break it down into manageably small pieces. Thus, the first book in this GramEd editing series* begins with the most important grammatical aspect for student writers of the English sentence: the verb. Why start with verbs? All grammar errors are not created nor weighted equally. Some grammar errors are only annoying to the reader while other errors completely destroy reader comprehension. Verbs are some of the most important words in any given sentence. If the action of the sentence is misunderstood, the entire sentence can be a shambles*. Once a writer's verbs are solid, other areas can be considered*. Thus, this series begins with the verb.

All grammar features have two aspects: form and function. The form is what the feature looks like: how it is formed or spelled. The function* is how the feature is used: what it means or its purpose in the sentence. Often form and function are covered simultaneously* when studying grammar. However, because verbs are so complicated and so very important, I have divided the form and function of verb instruction into two separate books. Moreover, since between the topics* of form and function, the form is the easier of the two to master, this first book of the series covers verb form. Thus, this book on *Advanced Verb Form* will cover only the formation of the various verbs, for example, what ending should be used on a gerund, what subject-verb agreement looks like, and what pattern pieces are required for the verb tense* and voice patterns.

Conversely, this book will not explain verb functions. There will be no instruction on when to use the various tenses or when the passive* voice is more appropriate than the active. While these are without a doubt essential lessons, they are lessons of verb function, so will be covered in the upcoming book *Editing Academic Texts: Advanced Verb Function*. This book will only pertain to verb form instruction and practice.

So, you've read the introduction, and now you are ready to start editing. Before you begin, I do suggest you go over the Editing Strategies in Chapter 2. There will probably be something new you haven't tried before! Review the grammar as needed. When you are ready, dive in and practice your editing!

Remember, this is advanced editing, which means the language, vocabulary, and general content are college level. If you don't know a vocabulary word that has an asterisk * or a ❖, you should. If there are other words you don't know, you might want to highlight them and look them up as well. The emphasis should be on verbs. Keep in mind that you will be working on and editing verb forms, not verb tenses, nouns, or other parts of speech.

It isn't where you come from; it's where you are going that counts.
~Ella Fitzgerald

I'm sure that with concentrated* practice, your verb form usage, thus your accumulated writing skill, will improve. If you have any questions or would like to tell me how you are doing, I'd love to hear from you. If you find an error or typo in the book and let me know, I'll give you a shout out in the next book! You can email me at ccundertree@gmail.com or contact* me on my website at www.ccundertree.com.

Ready then?? Let's get started!!

If you think you can, you're right.

and if you think you can't, you're right.

~ Mary Kay Ash

CHAPTER 2

EDITING STRATEGIES

Understanding Writing Processes

Understanding Grammar Errors

Understanding Editing Strategies

If we did all the things we are capable of doing,
we would literally astound ourselves.
~ Thomas Alva Edison

Understanding Writing Processes

The steps in writing well are often misunderstood. It is a common misconception that good writers sit down at the keyboard, and words flow from their brains down to the fingers and voila! A masterpiece is born. The reality, whether for a college class or for a book like this is very different from that pictured fantasy. In fact, writing is rewriting. Sometimes ideas do flow effortlessly, but most of the time writing is grueling* work. Getting the words on the paper is just the first step. After that comes revising, which is reworking the ideas and content of the text.

Then, finally, comes the editing. Editing is checking over all the specific details required by the language -- all those tricky rules and patterns that make good grammar seem impossible. Language needs to be checked and reviewed for all writers, from the novice to the professional. This stage is the one where students often fail because they do not spend the time to edit well, or if they do spend time, it is inefficiently spent. These strategies here in this book are designed for this final stage of writing: editing.

These editing strategies will work for you. They are not particularly difficult; however, using them effectively will be time-consuming. Nonetheless, like most things, the more you practice, the better and faster you will become!

Writing is the hardest work in the world not involving heavy lifting.

~ Pete Hamill

> **Study Tip**
>
> If you want to review model paragraph structures, you can use the Practice Edits as model academic examples for topics like summary or argument. You can see how writing about different genres*, like fiction or nonfiction, may vary. You can also note how quotes are used in academic writing. Check out Appendix F for information on paragraph types and content!

Understanding Grammar Errors

In your writing classes, do you spend a ton of time and exhaustive* effort to improve your writing? Because you are reading this book and practicing correcting verb form errors, I'm going to assume the answer is a resounding* yes! And yet, you still have those pesky errors! Despite your great care, your writing assignment grade is not what you expect or hope for! How exasperating* that must be! How frustrated you must feel! Believe me, I do empathize. Before you can master a subject, you have to understand it. Thus, to become a master editor, it is helpful to comprehend why errors occur in the first place!

Grammar errors can be classified into three causes. Each cause requires specific solutions to rectify* the problems, and applying the wrong solution to the problem will lead to frustration and a lack of improvement. Recognizing the reason for the grammar error will help you to use the most efficient solution for the mistake, ultimately* resulting in better writing. Let's take a few minutes to investigate* the causes of grammar error and the solutions for each.

Cause 1: Lack of Knowledge

The first and most obvious reason for making language errors in writing is that the words and rules for using the particular grammatical language aspect are unknown. This often occurs* when someone is beginning to learn to use the language or is attempting a more advanced grammatical feature* than previously* used.

English is no doubt a difficult language to apply at an academic level of writing. English has over 150,000 actively used words, and about 15% of those words are verbs. With 24 verb tenses plus the conditional, subjunctive, causative, and modals for the verbs, that is a lot of possible errors! Also, verbs can be used as nouns, adjectives, and even phrase particles! There are certainly many rules to know with general usage rules plus* specific rules for certain verbs. No wonder it is hard to keep up with all those rules! To overcome a lack of knowledge, one must study. The more precise* a person can be in directing the study, the more useful that study can be.

To address Cause 1, five common verb form student-problem areas will be briefly* reviewed. These mini review lessons will re-examine the basic rules for irregular verbs, incorrect verbals, subject-verb agreement, verb tense patterns, and verb pattern shifting problems. This basic review is by no means intended to be the last word on grammatical instruction. Many excellent grammar handbooks are available in print as are many fantastic free web resources if you would like more study. Also, let's not forget the power of classroom instruction. These lessons are only designed to provide a basic review, so don't hesitate to seek* more in-depth study if you think you need it!

Cause 2: Lack of Recognition

The second reason for making language errors in writing is that the error itself is not recognized by the writer. This occurs at every level in all student writing, both native and non-native writing alike. If you have studied language in a class or on your own, you probably know many of the basic rules this book will cover. However, you still make mistakes. Why is that? The reason is clear; you do not see or recognize your own mistakes in your writing.

Editing one's own work is absolutely one of the hardest things to do. A writer knows what he means to say, so he doesn't always notice that the words on the page are not exactly what he intends. Plus, a writer knows what she intends to say, so she doesn't always notice those small little errors that exist on the page. Lucky for you, there are helpful methods available that can enable you to recognize what is actually written on the page so that you can fix any errors you have made.

To address Cause 2, I have provided five specifically targeted editing strategies to help you learn to see the error being studied. Some techniques may be new while others you may have already tried. Even if you aren't initially* interested in a strategy, I encourage you to try them all before you reject* any of them! You can't have too many tools in your writing toolbox!

You will find that as you master these strategies, you will be able to more easily discern* what you actually wrote and can thus fix the errors you may have formed in your texts. None of these approaches* are particularly challenging; nevertheless*, students do not always choose to practice them. Why might that be? The reason is simple: editing effectively is very time-consuming. Truly, writing itself is extremely time-consuming. This leads us to the third and final cause for grammar error.

Cause 3: Lack of Time

The final reason for making language errors in writing is perhaps the most frustrating to overcome, yet the easiest to understand. Writing takes time, lots and lots of time. Good writing takes even more time. Excellent writing takes an outrageous amount of time! Student writers often have difficulty with the sheer* amount of time investment* that quality writing requires. It is even more time-consuming for developing writers or non-native speakers of a language to produce error-free grammar.

Generally speaking, the time spent polishing and editing your written language should be double the time spent writing the draft*. Therefore, if you spend an hour and a half writing a one-page paper, you should consequently* spend at least 3 hours editing it through checking your language and vocabulary. This time requirement is for an accomplished writer; a developing student writer may need to spend even more editing time. I can just hear you now exclaiming: What?? How can I possibly spend that much time?!?

One way to decrease editing time is to become more effective and faster at editing through the strategies given in this book. Although it will be time-consuming to develop your editing abilities, once you do, you will find that your editing goes more smoothly, takes less time, and produces better results. Nevertheless, error-free writing takes an interminable* amount of time. I have seen a great reluctance* on the part of students to spend the required amount of time to have good grammar. You must plan and give yourself enough time to edit whether you are a beginning writer, an advanced writer or an experienced professional* writer like myself.

Let's look at a very real example from my personal writing for you to consider. In May 2016, Coleman's Classroom published* my second book, *Get into Medical School: A Step-By-Step Guide to The Application Process.* I thought the book was finished in February when I did the final edit after a countless number of drafts and employed an editor to double check my grammar and content. As I made the suggested changes and fixed errors, I thought it was finished in March. As I continued to polish my language and edit my grammar and double check my format*, I thought it was finished in April. I submitted* my "final" book for review five times. The fifth time, I was finished! And then, I saw on page 128 a mistake that had to be fixed. Finally, on May 15, the final final review draft six was done. Or at least I was done. I am quite sure as people read the book, they will find a mistake here or there and let me know. What's the lesson to be learned here? No matter how much time you're spending, it's probably not enough! There is always something more to do with a project*, but ultimately, it must be submitted!

Here's the personal motto that I write by:

Good writing is never finished; it is only due!

To address Cause 3, you can spend time by practicing the fifty-three verb form editing paragraphs. To get the most practice, do them all. In contrast*, you may choose just to work on the sections* for which your verb form problems have been revealed* by an instructor or an assignment, or you may do the ones assigned* by your instructor for a class. Regardless, I highly suggest that everyone complete all exercises in Chapter 3: Irregular Review. This particular category* is a problem for all writers, native and non-native English speakers alike.

To get the most out of this book, I suggest you spend a sufficient* amount of time. Try the various editing strategies. Become proficient in their use. The more time you spend, the easier the activities will become, and a more productive editing process* will result. Ultimately, the better writer you will become in transforming into a better editor.

I didn't get here dreaming about it or thinking about it.
I got here by doing it.
~Estee Lauder

Understanding Editing Strategies

Each of these strategies has positive aspects. I encourage you to try them all. The more techniques you can employ, the more likely to succeed you will be!

Focus Practice

To focus means to concentrate the effort. Focusing on specific grammar forms will enable the student editor to see those errors better. The entire structure of this editing book enables focus as it limits the grammar errors to verb forms. Thus, while you use this book, focusing will be easy. However, in your own writing, it is probable that you will have other errors as well. Nevertheless, by directing your attention to these verb forms and focusing all your effort on them, your brain can zero in* on the specific rules and aspects of these features. When you work on your own papers, start with the focus you have developed through verb form editing. Eliminate* those potential* errors first. Eventually, you will find that you make less of those errors in the first place.

The structure of the Practice Edits has already been laid out to facilitate* your improvement in focused practice; with the given five specific edits for each of the review lessons, you can focus on that particular verb form aspect. Even when you are working on the Combined Editing Practice paragraphs, you are still actually focusing on verb form only. Focusing on specific areas of error can save a great deal of time and effort in the long run!

Decide what you want, decide what you are willing to exchange for it.
Establish your priorities and go to work.
~H. L. Hunt

Isolation is the single most effective method for identifying verb form errors. As you check for correct verb form, it is necessary to isolate and focus on the verbs in every sentence. When you are editing in this way, you are not reading the sentences for overall content meaning; instead, you are focused only on the verbs whether they are used as the main verb, as a gerund subject, or even as a participle adjective.

The first step is to assign an easy to recognize mark for the verbs. I personally like underlining because I am always in a hurry, and it is quick to underline something, but many of my students have found color highlighting* to be a more effective technique for them. In the given examples, underlining will be used to indicate the Isolation of the verb forms. After deciding how you prefer to identify your verbs, then look at the text.

In the case of this book's editing practice, each edit is only a paragraph, but when editing your own work, the text will probably be longer. In the text, look at each word, identifying the verbs and marking them in the way you have chosen. Of course, multi-clausal sentences will have more marks than simple clauses*. Every sentence should have at least one main verb marked. You may see multiple main verbs as the sentences get longer. You should also be able to identify those gerunds and verbal adjectives as well. Don't read for overall content or comprehension when editing verbs; instead, focus on the word-level errors.

After you have indicated all the verbs in the text, you will review the form of each verb, one by one. As you review each and every verb you have marked, review the rules as needed to check your comprehension. You will be amazed at how many errors you can catch and correct using this strategy!

As you edit, fix each mistake you discover. Then, go back and rewrite or retype your paper with these corrections if you are editing for a class. While using the Practice Edits herein, double check your corrections with the Suggested Answers after each edit. Review the Answers Explained section for the edit. Sometimes, more than one answer will be possible, but the given explanations will be the most obvious way to correct the error.

Let's see what this strategy looks like with an Academic Text from my book *An ESL Student's Guide to Good Communication with Classmates*. Review the following example of the Isolation Strategy with all verb forms underlined. Read the Verbs Explained. There are no errors in the following example. In the Verbs Explained, sentence subjects are italicized, and verb forms are bolded.

Isolation Technique Example – With No Errors
Academic Text
<u>Making</u> eye contact along with the smile <u>conveys</u> the message that all the attention <u>is</u> on you, the person <u>being looked</u> at. So many people today <u>are</u> <u>overlooked</u> or <u>misunderstood</u>. The actions of s<u>miling</u> and <u>meeting</u> eyes <u>say</u> that "I <u>see</u> you and <u>want to talk</u> with you!" These <u>are</u> powerful messages before words even <u>come</u> out of your mouth!
Underlined Verbs Explained
<ul><li>The gerund form *making* requires the singular verb form **conveys**.</li><li>The singular noun *attention* requires the singular verb form **is**.</li><li>The adjective form requires the present participle verb form **being**.</li><li>The plural verb form **are** with the past participles **overlooked** and **misunderstood** is required in this passive voice simple verb form pattern.</li><li>The plural noun *actions* requires the plural verb form **say**.</li><li>The pronoun *I* requires the singular verb forms **see** and **want**.</li><li>The plural pronoun *these* requires the plural verb form **are**.</li><li>The plural noun *words* requires the plural verb form **come**.</li></ul>

What really matters is what you do with what you have.
~Shirley Lord

So, that is what the strategy of Isolation looks like. Now let's read another example with verb form errors in the Academic Text. Note in the Verbs Explained, the correct verb form is bolded, and the nouns are italicized for ease of understanding. Review the Revised Text. See how easy it is to catch those tricky verb form errors using this method?

Isolation Strategy Example – With Errors
Academic Text
You <u>will</u> probably <u>be talk</u> to people in your class or in your environment. Even the elevator <u>provide</u> common ground. There <u>is</u> always common ground when you <u>are</u> in the same place at the same time. <u>Asking</u> "<u>did</u> you <u>do</u> the homework?" always <u>work</u> for a classmate. <u>Say</u> "elevators make me nervous!" <u>is</u> a nice general comment.
Underlined Verbs Explained
<ul><li>The present participle verb form **talking** is required in this active voice future continuous verb pattern.</li><li>The singular noun *elevator* requires the singular verb form **provides**.</li><li>The singular noun *ground* requires the singular verb form **is**.</li><li>The pronoun *you* requires the verb form **are**.</li><li>The gerund verb form *asking* requires the present participle.</li><li>The pronoun *you* requires irregular verb form **did**.</li><li>The gerund form *asking* requires the singular verb form **works**.</li><li>The gerund verb form *saying* requires the present participle.</li><li>The gerund verb form *saying* requires the singular irregular verb **is**.</li><li>The plural noun *elevators* requires the plural verb form **make**.</li></ul>
Text Revised
You **will** probably **be talking** to people in your class or in your environment. Even the elevator **provides** common ground. There **is** always common ground when you **are** in the same place at the same time. **Asking** "**did** you **do** the homework?" always **works** for a classmate. **Saying** "elevators **make** me nervous!" **is** a nice general comment.

The point then of the Isolation strategy is simply to accentuate and focus on the grammar under consideration. While this book is all about verb form and so this explanation has been directed at that grammatical aspect, the Isolation strategy works just as well with any aspect of grammar. Of all the techniques and tricks I teach in my writing classroom, this is by far the most effective one to learn. If you can find your errors, you can usually rectify them.

> **Study Tip**
>
> Focusing and Isolating errors, though time-consuming at first, will actually save you time in the long run. Moreover, the more you practice seeing the grammar in isolation, the more likely you will be to see any errors while you are writing them. If you are only going to try one strategy, Isolation should be the one!!

Read Aloud

Often times when editing, students just read the work over and over again. However, this strategy doesn't always serve well to find grammar errors, especially for non-native English speakers. Remember, one of the three reasons for grammar errors is that we don't see the error. Our brains are amazing machines that can add words that should be there even if they aren't. Thus, we have to compel* our eyes and brains to see what is in fact on the page, not just what should be on the page. If you realize you are missing some of the verbs when you read the practice edits, you might find the Read Aloud strategy to be helpful.

Reading aloud can be a very effective strategy if done correctly. The key to this technique is the speed of the reading. When reading out loud, don't try to hurry. Instead, slow down; read slowly. If you are not in a place where you can be talking to yourself, then just mouth the words. You should still hear them in your head. The physicality* of speaking the words even without sound will help you to find the mistakes.

As you read, identify the parts of speech, note what goes where, and make the effort to evaluate* your language. See what is on the page and then say what is on the page. Speak in a normal tone of voice so that you can hear your words out loud. The more English you have and use, the more your ears can help you find your mistakes.

Slow down!! Read slowly!!

Let's look at an example of this strategy in the Academic Text below. Note that the focus is on the verbs, which are underlined as part of the Isolation editing strategy. Then take a look at the Read Aloud Commentary. Even though I can't actually Read Aloud with you, I can demonstrate what reading aloud would look like through a realistic example text of what I would actually say as I Read Aloud. In the Read Aloud commentary example, I have bolded the Academic Text and italicized my own comments that I said as I read the text. To further make clear the text from my comments, I have begun and ended each of the italicized comments with a dash. The following example has no grammar errors.

Read Aloud Strategy Example – With No Errors
Academic Text
Friendship <u>takes</u> time <u>to develop</u>. <u>Don't</u> <u>get</u> <u>discouraged</u> if you <u>talk</u> to someone in class and <u>don't</u> <u>become</u> best buddies that same day. <u>Talk</u> to someone every day or every class. <u>Give</u> it time. <u>See</u> where the conversation <u>takes</u> you.
Read Aloud Commentary
Friendship takes - *yes that's 3rd person singular, so it needs an S* - **Friendship takes time to develop** – *to develop is the infinitive, and the form is right.* - **Don't get discouraged** – *don't that's the imperative verb form, so the subject is you. That's right. Discouraged needs the past participle here not the present discouraging.* - **Don't get discouraged if you talk to someone in class and don't become** – *talk shouldn't have an S because it agrees with second person you. Become is the base form that is used with the don't so that's right too* – **don't become best buddies that same day. Talk to someone every day or every class. Give it time.** - *Both of those sentences are the imperative you command form, 2nd person you, so the verb form is correct for subject-verb agreement.* - **See where the conversation takes you.** - *Again, see is imperative, so that's right. Conversation is 3rd person singular, so it takes the S. Good job me!*

Do you see, from the example, how analytical the reading should be? The goal of reading aloud is to carefully consider all the verbs, or whatever other feature is being analyzed. With this strategy, more words are actually better than less!

Let's look at another example, this time with some verb form errors.

Read Aloud Technique Example – With Errors
Academic Text
Friendships <u>is</u> like a flower. With the sunshine of positive conversation and the soil of common interest, the passage of time <u>present</u> beautiful results. Everyone <u>may</u> not <u>wants</u> <u>to be</u> your friend, but <u>would</u> you <u>want</u> to be friends with someone who <u>don't</u>? <u>Don't</u> <u>be</u> afraid to be you; there <u>are</u> people who <u>will cares</u> for you just as you <u>be</u>.
Read Aloud Commentary
Friendships is - *plural noun doesn't take S, so doesn't agree here. Because flower is singular, I'll make friendship singular too and keep the is.* - **Friendship is like a flower**. – *that's better. Good job me!* - **With the sunshine of positive conversation and the soil of common interest, the passage of time present** - *Present is a plural verb, but passage is singular; I need to change to presents.* – **The passage of time presents beautiful results. Everyone may not wants** –*No S marker allowed with the modal may. Change that. Nice catch!* – **but would you want to be friends with someone who don't** – *would want to be. Good. Someone is singular so who is singular so don't is wrong. It should be doesn't. Someone who doesn't.* – **don't be afraid** – *don't be, you don't be, yep!* – **don't be afraid to be you. There are people** – *people is plural, so there are people is right. Whoohoo!* – **there are people who will cares** – *Ugh! I did it again! No S marker with a modal. Be more careful with your modals girl!* – **who will care for you just as you be** – *I can't use base form be with you. I have to use are.* – **Who will care for you just as you are.** – *Finished! That was tough!*
Revised Text
Friendship **is** like a flower. With the sunshine of positive conversation and the soil of common interest, the passage of time **presents** beautiful results. Everyone **may** not **want to be** your friend, but **would** you **want** to be friends with someone who **doesn't**? **Don't be** afraid to be you; there **are** people who **will care** for you just as you **are**.

Goodness gracious! That seems like a lot of words and time for such a small sample, doesn't it? Now, you may be wondering if I would actually use all those words as I Read Aloud my work. The answer is a vehement* yes. Remember the goal is to go slowly as I have modeled. Did you notice that I praised myself for the things I did correctly? It is important to not just mention your errors but also focus on the positive* aspects of your writing as well. I guarantee* that you do many things correctly! Take pleasure in that even as you fix your mistakes.

Reading aloud can be an effective strategy to help you identify the errors in your work and correct them as you go. You might combine the Isolation strategy with the Read Aloud strategy. After you underline your verb forms, you might read the whole thing aloud, checking yourself as you go. Remember, the more strategies you incorporate, the more success you will have! Most importantly, for the Read Aloud strategy, you need to read slowly and deliberately!

Success isn't measured by the position you reach in life;
it's measured by the obstacles you overcome.
~Booker T. Washington

Take Breaks

Another strategy for effective editing is taking a break; unfortunately, this requires good time management skills. Many students work right up until the minute a paper is due. This could be occurring for several reasons such as the paper took longer than they expected, they are overwhelmed with the college workload, or perhaps they just waited until the last minute. This happens to everybody! One of the reasons working until the last minute is a bad idea is because when that occurs, the writer cannot employ this helpful technique of taking a break.

Taking a break is a straightforward process. It means to take some time away from your paper before you edit or in between edits. Writing is a cycle* – writing is rewriting! Your brain needs time to process in between the time of output* and time of editing. The more time you can give yourself in between writing and editing, the more effective your editing might be. Stop writing! Walk away from the computer or paper. Do something fun that has nothing to do with your writing. Once your brain is rested, then you can begin again.

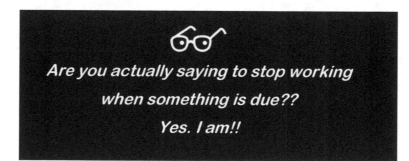

Are you actually saying to stop working when something is due??
Yes. I am!!

How much time you can take off depends on how much time you have budgeted for the project at hand. If your work is due the next day, you have very little time to work with, but if you have days or a week, then you can take more time off. In the process of writing this book, I took several breaks from the computer. I went to the beach with Mr. C, I read some new fiction, and I watched a new series on Netflix. I did many things that had nothing to do with writing or grammar or editing. When I came back to the book after resting, I saw the material with new eyes and a new perspective*; this made me fresher and ready to begin again.

You can do the same thing even for the paragraph edits in this book. Once you have finished your Isolation and Reading Aloud and before you check the suggested answers, take a quick break. Even five or ten minutes can be useful. Check your Facebook or text a friend. Then, give the edit one more go. You might be surprised at what you find the second time.

Success is no accident. It is hard work, perseverance, learning, studying, sacrifice and most of all, love of what you are doing or learning to do.
~Pele

Have Fun

The absolute best yet perhaps hardest strategy for editing is to have fun. For most writers, even myself sometimes, this can be an unattainable* idea. Think of the adjectives you would use to describe editing. Many students have used frustrating, painful, baffling*, stressful*... rarely ever does anyone think fun. Why should we and how can we make editing fun?

People learn better when the task* is enjoyable; few would dispute* this fact. Educators spend countless hours trying to ascertain* just how to make tedious tasks like editing fun. Personally, I think attitude* is what makes things interesting and fun. If you dread editing, if you don't want to do it, or if you put it off until the last minute, then you won't have any fun doing it. I'm not trying to suggest that developing your editing skills will ever be as fun as say having lunch with a friend or watching the new summer blockbuster. Nonetheless*, being good at something in and of itself can be a satisfying reward.

One way that I personally try to make editing fun is by keeping score of my corrections. When I edit my own work, I count how many errors I discern. Rather than being upset at these errors, and I do discover errors, I count them as I go. I basically keep a score card of my errors. I total them up at the end. Then I congratulate myself for all of those errors that I fixed on my own. Sometimes I give myself a reward like $.50 for every error and then I buy something fun with the money I've earned. Of course, it's not fun to have errors. However, catching my own errors and correcting them before anyone else sees them, that is gratifying*. Maybe you could have some favorite music that you listen to as you work or give yourself a treat when you spend enough time editing. There is no one way to have fun. One thing I know for sure is that if you can make editing enjoyable at some level, you will get better, be more effective, and do a better job!

You may find some strategies work better in certain situations or with certain errors. I use all these strategies in my own writing, but for different purposes. For example, I generally Focus on one section of my work at a time. I use Isolation with the nitty-gritty* kind of errors for me, like punctuation and MLA, and I Read Aloud with all my major* content. Taking breaks helps me to see the words on the paper more easily. Finally, Having Fun with my writing and editing helps the whole process move more smoothly.

The best strategy is using the most appropriate* tool for the job at hand. Therefore, you need to have multiple ways to approach your editing. Being a good editor just takes good strategy and loads of time. I know that you can become one if you work at it! Practicing these strategies with the Practice Edits will give you a good start to master these techniques and become a better editor for your own work!

If you don't like something, change it;
if you can't change it,
change the way you think about it.
~Mary Engelbreit

Study Tip

Identifying the cause of your error will help you quickly resolve it. Are you making mistakes because you lack knowledge of that grammar feature? Take the time to learn it. Are you making mistakes despite knowing the grammar rules because you didn't see the actual mistake? Learn to see your own errors in your work. Are you doing your best but still making multiple mistakes? Spend more time; you can always spend more! Identifying the cause of your grammar error and applying the best solution will help you become an excellent editor and writer!

Editing Strategies Summary

- Understand the cyclical nature of academic writing.
- Understand the three reasons for grammar errors and apply the best solution for each.
- Focus on one grammar feature at a time to develop your editing skills. Once you know your particular errors, you can always focus on that particular grammar feature.
- Isolate the specific feature that you're working on by marking it in some way and then checking your work for that particular feature without worrying about the overall* content.
- Read aloud through slow and deliberate examination of the individual* words in your text. Make sure that you analyze what you're doing as you go.
- Take a break from your writing and editing to give your mind some relaxation* and refresh your ideas.
- Have fun in some small way to mitigate the stress of error correction.
- Editing is an integral* part of writing; the better you are at editing, the better your writing will be!

Failure is the opportunity to begin again more intelligently.

~Henry Ford

3

IRREGULAR REVIEW

Grammar Review

5 Practice Edits

You can't try to do things

you simply must do them.

~ Ray Bradbury

Irregular Verb Forms

Every English verb has four forms: the base form, the present participle form, the past form, and the past participle form. Also, there are two kinds of verbs: regular and irregular. Take a look at Chart 1 below.

1. Base Form will be abbreviated as BF.

2. Present tense will be abbreviated as PRS.

3. Participle will be abbreviated as PART.

4. Past will be abbreviated as PST.

CHART 1: REGULAR AND IRREGULAR VERB FORM PATTERNS

REGULAR VERB FORM		IRREGULAR VERB FORM	
BF[1]	Verb	BF	Verb
PRS[2] PART[3]	Verb + ING	PRS PART	Verb + ING
PST[4]	Verb + ED	PST	Varies
PST PART	Verb + ED	PST PART	Varies

As you can see from the chart* above, the irregular verb form problem areas are in the past form and past participle. While there are some common formation patterns among the irregular verb forms, they do vary* a great deal. It is best to memorize these verbs one by one. A chart of the irregular verbs used in this book is given in Appendix D.

Fortunately, most of the verbs in English are regular with only approximately* 200 irregular verbs commonly used in modern English. Unfortunately, these irregular verbs are utilized for common actions, like reading, going, and eating; moreover, the auxiliary verbs forming the basis of the verb tense patterns, negative actions, interrogative questions, and subject verb agreement are also irregular. Hence*, the irregular verb patterns can cause many grammar form errors.

Regular verbs follow set rules!! Irregular verb rules vary!!

The English auxiliary verbs used for the tense patterns, negative forms, and question patterns are all irregular and indicated in the Chart 2.

Chart 2: Irregular Auxiliary Verbs

BF	PRS PART	PST FORM	PST PART
be	being	was / were	been
have	having	had	had
do	doing	did	done

These irregular auxiliary atypical* verbs must be memorized and used correctly since they are the basis for much of the verb usage. If you don't feel 100% confident in your ability to correctly use the verbs in the above chart, I highly suggest you take the time to feel comfortable with them. These verbs absolutely must be formed correctly if you want readers to take your writing seriously.

Some of the most commonly used daily verbs are irregular. Review the brief list below in Chart 3: Common Irregular Verbs. Do you see any patterns there?

Note how the irregular past participles end with an -N, -T, or -GHT rather than -ED. Also, *cut* has no change in the past form or past participle. Truly, the only way to master these irregular verb forms is to memorize them individually!

Chart 3: Common Irregular Verbs

BF	PRS PART	PST FORM	PST PART
write	writing	wrote	written
see	seeing	saw	seen
feel	feeling	felt	felt
cut	cutting	cut	cut
teach	teaching	taught	taught
think	thinking	thought	thought

With irregular verb forms, you must recognize errors with spelling or endings. Review the example errors, explanations, and revisions* of the following sentences.

Irregular Verb Form Examples

error	Yesterday, I **thinked** I would skip class.
explained	The past verb form **thought** is required by this irregular verb.
revised	Yesterday, I **thought** I would skip class.
error	The student **feeled** great when he **be** writing.
explained	The past form **felt** is required by this irregular verb. The past form **was** is required by this irregular verb.
revised	The student **felt** great when he **was** writing.
error	She **become** very tired since she had **drived** for hours.
explained	The past form **became** is required by this irregular verb. The past participle **driven** is required by this irregular verb.
revised	She **became** very tired since she had **driven** for hours.

Irregular and Regular Verb Form Summary

- Both regular and irregular verbs follow the same pattern with the base form.
- Regular and irregular verbs follow the same pattern with the present participle pattern.
- The base forms of most English verbs regularly follow the pattern of adding an –ED ending to the past and past participle forms.
- Some irregular verbs have varying past and past participle verb forms.
- While there are a few patterns for irregular verbs, mostly they have to be memorized.
- Irregular verb forms must be used correctly in academic writing.

Irregular Verb Form Practice Edits

Try one of the suggested Editing Strategies for these five irregular verb form edits. The best one, one according to my students, is the isolating of specific errors. In this case, look at any past tense or past participle verbs to check for irregular or regular verb form. You may also see some errors in the present tense with the three irregular auxiliary verbs. Keep in mind that not all verbs are irregular, so be careful not to apply irregular forms to regular verbs. Upon completion of these Practice Edits, make sure that you check your answers too! A great part of learning is recognizing our mistakes and learning from them.

Edit 1: Irregular Verb Forms
find and fix 5 verb form errors

In "So You've Got a Writing Assignment. Now What?," Corrine E. Hinton advises against procrastination. She states that "waiting until the last minute to complete a writing assignment in college is a gamble. You put yourself at risk for the unexpected" (Hinton 20). How true that is! If I had a dollar for every student whose internet failed at the last minute or who runed out of ink and couldn't print the paper, I could retire today. Of course, sometimes truly unexpected things do happen like getting an emergency telephone call from a faraway family member. However, some problems should be expected because technology will fail, people will oversleep, and traffic accidents will occur. Accounting for such circumstances is the mark of a mature, experienced student. How then can the unexpected be planned for? One thing I've always doed is set artificial deadlines for my work. For example, last weekend, I was grading my class's diagnostic essays and their new assignment beed due Monday at midnight, so my true deadline for getting the assignments graded was Monday morning. However, I set an earlier deadline for Sunday afternoon that way I could be sure to get them back on time. Unfortunately, I didn't meet my deadline because something unexpected comed up with Mr. C. I was not able to finish grading the assignments until Monday morning. In reality, though, this was still well within the final deadline that I had set, so I still safely meeted my deadline.

Edit 1: Suggested Answers

answers indicated in bold

In "So You've Got a Writing Assignment. Now What?," Corrine E. Hinton advises against procrastination. She states that "waiting until the last minute to complete a writing assignment in college is a gamble. You put yourself at risk for the unexpected" (Hinton 20). How true that is! If I had a dollar for every student whose internet failed at the last minute or who [1]**ran** out of ink and couldn't print the paper, I could retire today. Of course, sometimes truly unexpected things do happen like getting an emergency telephone call from a faraway family member. However, some problems can and should be expected because technology* will fail, people will oversleep, traffic accidents will occur, and accounting for such circumstances is the mark of a mature*, experienced student. How then can the unexpected be planned for? One thing I've[2] always **done** is set artificial deadlines for my work. For example, last weekend, I was grading my class's diagnostic essays and their new assignment [3]**was** due Monday at midnight, so my true deadline for getting the assignments graded was Monday morning. However, I set an earlier deadline for Sunday afternoon that way I could be sure to get them back on time. Unfortunately, I didn't meet my deadline because something unexpected [4]**came** up with Mr. C. I was not able to finish grading the assignments until Monday morning. In reality, though, this was still well within the final deadline that I had set, so I still safely [5]**met** my deadline.

Answers Explained

1. The past verb form **ran** is required by this irregular verb.
2. The past participle verb form **done** is required by this irregular verb.
3. The past verb form **was** is required by this irregular verb.
4. The past participle verb form **came** is required by this irregular verb.
5. The past verb form **met** is required by this irregular verb.

Edit 2: Irregular Verb Forms
find and fix 5 verb form errors

While *The Ancient Mariner* can be readed as a spooky intense mythic fable, its symbols also encourage other possible interpretations. Because Coleridge was a professed Christian, the poem is often explained as a Christian allegory. Coleridge speaked widely of many of his Christian beliefs. He said in a letter writted just after the completion of *The Ancient Mariner*, "I believe most steadfastly in original sin" (Warren 24). Moreover, Coleridge adamantly moralized the Christian idea of the fall of man, stating, "A Fall of some sort or other...is the fundamental postulate of the moral history of Man. Without this hypothesis, Man is unintelligible; with it, every phenomenon is explicable" (Warren 25). The Biblical notion of man's fall from grace beed clearly a foundation for Coleridge's sense of reality. Coleridge's statements on his Christian beliefs have leaded many to interpret the symbolism of *The Ancient Mariner* as a spiritual journey with "religious and moral allusions" in a Christian plot with "moral error, the discipline of suffering, and a consequent change of heart" (Perkins). The poem's symbols are clearly linked with the Biblical notion of sin and redemption through Christ.

Edit 2: Suggested Answers
answers indicated in bold

While *The Ancient Mariner* [1]**can be read** as a spooky intense mythic* fable, its symbols* also encourage other possible interpretations. Because Coleridge was a professed Christian, the poem is often explained as a Christian allegory. Coleridge [2]**spoke** widely of many of his Christian beliefs. He said in a letter [3]**written** just after the completion of *The Ancient Mariner,* "I believe most steadfastly in original sin" (Warren 24). Moreover, Coleridge adamantly moralized the Christian idea of the fall of man, stating, "A Fall of some sort or other…is the fundamental* postulate of the moral history of Man. Without this hypothesis*, Man is unintelligible; with it, every phenomenon* is explicable" (Warren 25). The Biblical notion of man's fall from grace [4]**was** clearly a foundation* for Coleridge's sense of reality. Coleridge's statements on his Christian beliefs have [5]**led** many to interpret the symbolism of *The Ancient Mariner* as a spiritual journey with "religious and moral allusions" in a Christian plot with "moral error, the discipline of suffering, and a consequent change of heart" (Perkins). The poem's symbols are clearly linked* with the Biblical notion* of sin and redemption through Christ.

Answers Explained

1. The past participle verb form **read** is required by this irregular verb.
2. The past form of the verb form **spoke** is required by this irregular verb.
3. The past participle verb form **written** is required by this irregular verb.
4. The past form verb form **was** is required by this irregular verb.
5. The past participle verb form **led** is required by this irregular verb.

Edit 3: Irregular Verb Forms
find and fix 4 verb form errors

In "Second Kind of Mind," JeVon Tompson argues that the belief in an idea, more than the actual truth of the

idea, is what leads to results. Tompson tells the story of being mathematically impaired all throughout school and

how this deficiency almost prevented him from getting his college degree. Luckily for him, he had Professor Fine,

who convinced him with his "second kind of mind" that he would get an A in his required statistics class because

he had already failed algebra three times. According to Fine, those minds that don't get algebra can ace statistics.

Tompson embraced this idea and changed his attitude about statistics; he beginned talking about how he would

not just pass, but excel in the class, he sitted in the front row of class and studied incessantly, and he even gived

up hanging out with his friends to work with a tutor. With all of this effort, he earned an A. At the end of the

semester, Tompson learned that Professor Fine would often trick the "slow students" with the second kind of

mind story, but it workt most times. The lesson of his story is that a person can achieve what may seem

impossible if the belief in the possibility of the achievement is there. People will become what they believe that

they can be whether that belief is true or not!

Edit 3: Suggested Answers

answers indicated in bold

In "Second Kind of Mind," JeVon Tompson argues that the belief in an idea more than the actual truth of the idea is what leads to results. Tompson tells the story of being mathematically impaired all throughout school and how this deficiency almost prevented him from getting his college degree. Luckily for him, he had Professor Fine, who convinced* him with his "second kind of mind" he would get an A in his required statistics* class because he had already failed algebra three times. According to Fine, those minds that don't get algebra can ace statistics. Tompson embraced this idea and changed his attitude about statistics; he ¹**began** talking about how he would not just pass, but excel in the class, he ²**sat** in the front row of class and studied incessantly, and he even ³**gave** up hanging out with his friends to work with a tutor. With all of this effort, he earned an A. At the end of the semester, Tompson learned that Professor Fine would often trick the "slow students" with the second kind of mind story, but it ⁴**worked** most times. The lesson of his story is that a person can achieve* what may seem impossible if the belief in the possibility of the achievement is there. People will become what they believe they can be whether that belief is true or not!

Answers Explained

1. The past verb form **began** is required by this irregular verb.
2. The past verb form **sat** is required by this irregular verb.
3. The past verb form **gave** is required by this irregular verb.
4. The past verb form **worked** is required by this regular verb.

Edit 4: Irregular Verb Forms
find and fix the verb form errors

Poetry often makes an argument through asking questions as does the poem titled

"Harlem" by Langston Hughes, where he asks what happens when a dream is setted aside. By

implying unfavorable answers to these questions, he subtly makes an argument about the risks

of giving up dreams. Does a delayed dream "dry up like a raisin in the sun" or "stink like rotten

meat?" asks Hughes. Does this holded-up dream "sag" or does it ultimately "explode?"

(Hughes). All the possibilities gived for this deferred dream are clearly negative. Never does

Hughes suggest that waiting on a dream might actually make it stronger or greater. Clearly,

Hughes is arguing that having an unfulfillen dream would be a negative circumstance. I agree

that having unfulfillen dreams can lead to life explosions in bitterness and anger, yet I think

Hughes' choice of the word "defer" is an often overlooked aspect of this poem. He isn't

discussing a rejected or forgetted dream, just a delayed dream. Sometimes, dreams can be like

fine wines, the more they age, they better they can be. Sometimes also, dreams can change

while in a holding pattern. I would find this poem to be more compelling if it were about a

dream deleted rather than deferred.

Edit 4: Suggested Answers
answers indicated in bold

Poetry often makes an argument through asking questions as does the poem titled "Harlem" by Langston Hughes, where he asks what happens when a dream is [1]**set** aside. By implying* unfavorable answers to these questions, he subtly makes an argument about the risks of giving up dreams. Does a delayed dream "dry up like a raisin in the sun" or "stink like rotten meat?" asks Hughes. Does this [2]**held**-up dream "sag" or does it ultimately "exlode?" (Hughes). All the possibilities [3]**given** for this deferred dream are clearly negative. Never does Hughes suggest that waiting on a dream might actually make it stronger or greater. Clearly, Hughes is arguing that having an [4]**unfulfilled** dream would be a negative circumstance. I agree that having unfulfilled dreams can lead to life explosions in bitterness and anger, yet I think Hughes' choice of the word "defer" is an often overlooked aspect of this poem. He isn't discussing a rejected or [5]**forgotten** dream, just a delayed dream. Sometimes, dreams can be like fine wines: the more they age, they better they can be. Sometimes, also, dreams can change while in a holding pattern. I would find this poem to be more compelling if it were about a dream deleted rather than deferred.

Answers Explained

1. The past verb form **set** is required by this irregular verb.
2. The past verb form **held** is required by this irregular verb.
3. The past participle verb form **given** is required by this irregular verb.
4. The past verb form **unfulfilled** is required by this regular verb.
5. The past participle verb form **forgotten** is required by this irregular verb.

Edit 5: Irregular Verb Forms
find and fix the verb form errors

It has been a confusing time in the recent American society. Politicians daily flinged insults back and forth, and mass shootings have become more commonplace. What to believe and how to express those beliefs is becoming even more difficult to figure out. Ted Gup, in "In Praise of the Wobblies," suggests that it is alright to be indecisive sometimes. He argues that is "okay to be perplexen, to be torn by issues, to look at the world and not feel inadequate because it would not sort itself out cleanly" (Gup 98). Basically, Gup affirms the idea that the world does not always divide neatly into precisely identifiable categories. This notion may be particularly relevant to today's college ESL student who often feels teared between two or more cultures, ideologies, and languages. Students trying to most effectively improve their writted and speaked usage of English must embrace the language and culture wholeheartedly, yet the very action of improvement may be viewed as a rejection of their original culture and language. Moreover, American college classes will introduce new and perhaps even culturally loathed ideologies for non-natives and natives alike in the examination of concepts of equality and freedom that not everyone agrees with. It is important, then, to realize that being confusen is not necessarily a bad thing. Gup states he accepted his confusion as a friend and ally with no apologies needed. It may just be the "open-minded, inquisitive, and, yes, confused" who provide a common ground for others (Gup 99).

Edit 5: Suggested Answers

answers indicated in bold

It has been a confusing time in the recent American society. Politicians have daily [1]**flung** insults back and forth, and mass shootings have become more commonplace. What to believe and how to express those beliefs is becoming even more difficult to figure out. Ted Gup, in "In Praise of the Wobblies," suggests that it is alright to be indecisive sometimes. He argues that is "okay to be [2]**perplexed**, to be torn by issues*, to look at the world and not feel inadequate* because it would not sort itself out cleanly" (Gup 98). Basically, Gup affirms the idea that the world does not always neatly divide into precisely identifiable categories. This notion may be particularly relevant to today's college ESL student who often feels [3]**torn** between two or more cultures*, ideologies*, and languages. Students trying to most effectively improve their [4]**written** and [5]**spoken** usage of English must embrace the language and culture wholeheartedly, yet the very action of improvement may be viewed as a rejection of their original culture and language. Moreover, American college classes will introduce new and perhaps even culturally loathed* ideologies for non-natives and natives alike in the examination of concepts of equality and freedom that not everyone agrees with. It is important, then, to realize that being [6]**confused** is not necessarily a bad thing. Gup states he accepted his confusion as a friend and ally with no apologies needed. It may just be the "open-minded, inquisitive, and, yes, confused" who provide a common ground for others (Gup 99).

Answers Explained

1. The past verb form **flung** is required by this irregular verb.
2. The past participle verb form **perplexed** is required by this regular verb.
3. The past participle verb form **torn** is required by this irregular verb.
4. The past participle verb form **written** is required by this irregular verb.
5. The past participle verb form **spoken** is required by this irregular verb.
6. The past participle verb form **confused** is required by this regular verb.

VERBAL REVIEW

Grammar Review

5 Practice Edits

Mistakes are portals of discovery.

~James Joyce

Verb Forms

Verbs can be used as nouns and modifiers with specific verb forms; these non-verbs are often called verbals. For this brief review, three kinds of verbal forms will be considered: gerunds, simple adjectives, and participial modifiers.

Gerunds

Verbs used as nouns are called gerunds. Any English verb can become a gerund with the addition of -ING to the base form verb, which is the same form as the present participle. Gerunds are primarily singular nouns, never plural. There are exceptions to every rule in English, but for the most part, you will never write a plural gerund. Thus, a plural marker is almost never used with a gerund.

The patterns of gerunds as subject, object, and object of preposition are indicated in Chart 4.

CHART 4: GERUND VERBAL PATTERNS

NOUN SUBJECT	NOUN OBJECT	NOUN OBJECT OF PREP
Editing well is tough.	I enjoy **editing**.	Strategies for **editing** are useful.
Writing rules matter.	She loves **writing**.	I like learning about **writing**.

Review the examples of errors, explanations, and revisions in the following Gerund examples.

Gerund Verb Form Examples

error	**Improve** one's writing requires dedication and effort.
explained	The gerund form requires the present participle **improving**.
revised	**Improving** one's writing requires dedication and effort.
error	I enjoy **read** historical fiction.
explained	The gerund form requires the present participle **reading**.
revised	I enjoy **reading** historical fiction.
error	**Editings** effectively are important aspects of college **writings**.
explained	The gerund form requires the present participle **editing**. The gerund form requires the present participle **writing**.
revised	**Editing** effectively is an important aspect of college **writing**.

Study Tip

Some gerund nouns have become such a part of the general vocabulary that they are no longer even considered gerunds, for example, feelings. While feel is, of course, a verb, the noun "feelings" is usually used in the plural form as in "Please, don't hurt my feelings because I am very sensitive." Keep in mind that this plural gerund is the exception to the rule and very rare. In general, gerunds are never plural!

Simple Adjectives

Present and past participles used as adjectives are another category of verbals. These simple adjectives are generally one-word adjectives like the regular adjective happy or sad. Unlike a regular adjective, however, these simple verbal adjectives are a present or past verb participle.

When choosing between the present participle and the past participle form, it is important to consider the noun being modified. As a present participle is active, it modifies a noun doing an action while the past participle is more passive, so it modifies a noun that is receiving the action by or feeling from something else. Thus in an interesting class, the class itself is interesting; however, in an interested class, the class is being interested in a teacher or activity.

Just like the regular adjective, these single-word adjective verbals are usually placed directly before the noun being modified. Remember, it is important for the past participle to utilize the correct form with any irregular verbs.

The patterns of single-word verbals as simple adjectives are indicated in Chart 5.

CHART 5: SINGLE-WORD ADJECTIVE VERBAL PATTERNS

REGULAR ADJ	PRS PART	REGULAR PST PART	IRREGULAR PST PART
happy	verb + ING	verb + ED	various forms
happy woman The woman herself is **happy**.	**interesting** topic The topic itself is **interesting** because of its content.	**interested** student The student is made **interested** or feels **interested** because of something else.	**written** word The word was **written** by someone else.

Review the following examples with confused present or past participles.

Simple Verbal Adjective Examples

error	The **tiring** teacher wearily walked to her car after class.
explained	The teacher is clearly feeling something (exhaustion) and was made to feel this way by something else (probably her students), so this adjective verb form requires the past participle **tired**.
revised	The **tired** teacher wearily walked to her car after class.
error	The **fascinated** novel will intrigue my ESL students.
explained	A novel can't feel fascinated, so this adjective verb form requires the present participle **fascinating**.
revised	The **fascinating** novel will intrigue my ESL students.
error	The **boring** students make the instructor work harder to engage them in the **interested** curriculum.
explained	When students feel bored and are not engaged, the teacher must work harder; so this adjective form requires the past participle **bored**. A curriculum can't feel interested in something, so this adjective form requires the present participle **interesting**.
revised	The **bored** students make the instructor work harder to engage them in the **interesting** curriculum.

Besides choosing the wrong ending with a past or present participle, other participle form errors occur when the base form instead of the particle or the wrong irregular/regular form is used.

Review the examples below of correct and incorrect verbal adjective form usage.

More Simple Verbal Adjective Examples

error	Memorizing provides **remember** facts; analyzing helps with **knowed** ones.
explained	The adjective form requires the past participle **remembered**. The adjective form requires the irregular past participle **known**.
revised	Memorizing provides **remembered** facts; analyzing helps with **known** ones.

Phrasal Adjectives

Unlike the simple verbal adjectives, the phrasal adjectives are more complex, usually including multiple words in the adjective phrase such as a direct object or a prepositional phrase. The modifying phrases can be placed before the noun like the single-word modifiers or after the noun being modified similar* to a relative pronoun adjective clause.

Take a look at Chart 6 for example patterns.

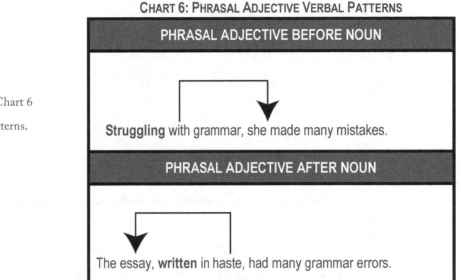

CHART 6: PHRASAL ADJECTIVE VERBAL PATTERNS

PHRASAL ADJECTIVE BEFORE NOUN

Struggling with grammar, she made many mistakes.

PHRASAL ADJECTIVE AFTER NOUN

The essay, **written** in haste, had many grammar errors.

The important thing to be aware* of is the participle formation rules don't change, so you must use the correct endings with these adjective verbals. Review the following examples.

Phrasal Verbal Adjective Examples

error	**Try** all the editing strategies, she was able to improve.
explained	The adjective form requires the present participle **trying**.
revised	**Trying** all the editing strategies, she was able to improve.
error	The textbook, **choose** by Prof. Undertree, facilitated student learning.
explained	The adjective form requires the past participle **chosen**.
revised	The textbook, **chosen** by Prof. Undertree, facilitated student learning.

Verbal Form Review

- Gerunds use the present participle form.

- Gerunds are almost never plural.

- Gerunds can be used as noun subjects, objects, or objects of prepositions.

- Single-word verbal adjectives can be either present or past participles.

- Phrasal adjectives can be either present or past participles.

- All regular past participles end in –ED

- Irregular past participles forms vary.

- The present and past participle have different meanings so choose carefully!

Study Tip

Spend some time and energy to understand the attributes of the present participle and the past participle. If you need to, review them more deeply. The meanings of the present participle and of the past participle are not identical! A mistake in verb form from one to the other causes an unwanted mistake in meaning. Be careful!

Verbal Verb Forms Practice Edits

Try one of the suggested Editing Strategies for these five practice edits with missing or incorrect endings in these verbal form edits. You might try the strategy of reading aloud here. If you use isolation of errors, make sure that you consider all the verbs in the sentence. Remember, the focus on these Practice Edits is gerunds and participle adjectives. Also, be aware that these errors can occur in any part of the paragraphs, even the quotations!

Edit 6: Verbal Forms
find and fix 4 verb form errors

William Faulkner's use of point of view in the heartbreak short story "Barn Burning" enables the reader to agonize with Snopes as he makes decisions about his father. Snopes is torn between his conscience and the ties of blood demanded by his father. Snopes has been taught that Justice is "our enemy… mine and hisn both" even though his father is committing crimes (Faulkner 3). The revelation of Snopes' thoughts enables the reader to feel connected with Snopes' overwhelm emotions and feel his pain. Faulkner further develops this pain of indecision when Snopes realizes "I could run on and on, and never look back, never need to see [my father's] face again. Only I can't. I can't" (Faulkner 21). Snopes is trapped in his mind with the pain of disagree with his father's actions while the ties of blood demand his loyalty. The first person narrator enables the reader to connect with Snopes' pain to bring the reader into the Snope' s dilemma of do what is right for the family or right for humanity.

Edit 6: Suggested Answers
answers indicated in bold

William Faulkner's use of point of view in the [1]**heartbreaking** short story "Barn Burning" enables the reader to agonize with Snopes as he makes decisions about his father. Snopes is torn between his conscience and the ties of blood demanded by his father. Snopes has been taught that Justice is "our enemy… mine and hisn both" even though his father is committing* crimes (Faulkner 3). The revelation of Snopes' thoughts enables the reader to feel connected with Snopes' [2]**overwhelming** emotions and feel his pain. Faulkner further develops this pain of indecision when Snopes realizes "I could run on and on, and never look back, never need to see [my father's] face again. Only I can't. I can't" (Faulkner 21). Snopes is trapped in his mind with the pain of [3]**disagreeing** with his father's actions while the ties of blood demand his loyalty. The first person narrator enables the reader to connect with Snopes' pain to bring the reader into the Snope' s dilemma of [4]**doing** what is right for the family or right for humanity.

Answers Explained

1. The adjective form requires the present participle **heartbreaking**.
2. The adjective form requires the present participle **overwhelming**.
3. The gerund form requires the present participle **disagreeing**.
4. The gerund form requires the present participle **doing**.

Edit 7: Verbal Forms
find and fix 4 verb form errors

Even though instruction incorporate various learning styles is clearly important, implanting these differing styles is not easy. For instance, in 1987 the New York school district printed an educational pamphlet listing learning style differences to reduce the dropout rate of African-American students. However, these differences were interpreted as "explanations for deficits" in the educational system and stirred up a debate about "educational equity" (Guild 53-54). The truth of the vary learning styles was submerged under the educational debate between the melt pot and cultural pluralism (Guild). Other valid reasons that learning style variations cannot be incorporated into the classroom are that various styles cannot solve all possible learning problems; plus, teachers might not be able to use styles that they do not embrace and most educators want to facilitate, structure, and validate successful learning for all students (Guild). Most also agree to some degree that learning styles and cultural differences play an important role in that successful process. Thus, completely overthrow the current system is an impractical and unpleasant idea, yet some modifications could be and should be made to include the various learning styles and improve the educational experiences for all students.

Edit 7: Suggested Answers

answers indicated in bold

Even though instruction [1]**incorporating** various learning styles* is clearly important, implanting these differing styles is not easy. For instance*, in 1987 the New York school district printed an educational pamphlet listing learning style differences to reduce the dropout rate of African-American students. However, these differences were interpreted as "explanations for deficits" in the educational system and stirred up a debate* about "educational equity" (Guild 53-54). The truth of the [2]**varied** learning styles was submerged under the educational debate between the [3]**melting** pot and cultural pluralism (Guild). Other valid* reasons that learning style variations cannot be incorporated into the classroom are that various styles cannot solve all possible learning problems; plus, teachers might not be able to use styles that they do not embrace and most educators want to facilitate, structure, and validate successful learning for all students (Guild). Most also agree to some degree that learning styles and cultural differences play an important role* in that successful process. Thus, completely [4]**overthrowing** the current system is an impractical and unpleasant idea, yet some modifications could be and should be made to include the various learning styles and improve the educational experiences for all students.

Answers Explained

1. The adjective form requires the present participle **incorporating**.
2. The adjective form requires the past participle **varied**.
3. The adjective form requires the present participle **melting**.
4. The gerund form requires the present participle **overthrowing**.

Edit 8: Verbal Forms
find and fix 4 verb form errors

An enhance change in her type of motivation was a definite factor in Jodee Blanco's ultimate

success. Blanco was excessively bullied by her classmates; this outside influence undoubtedly caused

her to want to change her circumstances as she sought to be accepted not only by her peers but also her

parents. She explained how she was "anxious to show [her] parents the proof that [she] was no longer a

misfit" (Blanco 53). Blanco was, in fact, addressing the larger matter of external motivation. Daniel

Pink argued that such motivation is a type of stick or punishment and works for algorithmic tasks;

unfortunately, the make of friends and finding one's place in a social group is not really a task in which

one can "follow a set of establish instructions down a single pathway to one conclusion," which is how

algorithmic activities succeed (15). Thus, this kind of debilitate motivation led Blanco to further

heartache with her hostile, cruel classmates. While the external motivation did not lead to success, when

Blanco changed her perspective and her motivation became internal, she began to experience success as

she realized that her negative experiences were actually a strength. Blanco realized that "I'm one of the

lucky ones because I'm full of hope for the future" (245). Her new motivation was rather heuristic

because she had to "experiment with possibilities and devise a novel solution" (Pink 16). It was this

very change from the extrinsic to the intrinsic motivation that enabled her to overcome her past.

Edit 8: Suggested Answers

answers indicated in bold

An [1]**enhancing** change in her type of motivation was a definite factor* in Jodee Blanco's ultimate success. Blanco was excessively bullied by her classmates; this outside influence undoubtedly caused her to want to change her circumstances as she sought to be accepted not only by her peers but also her parents. She explained how she was "anxious to show [her] parents the proof that [she] was no longer a misfit" (Blanco 53). Blanco was, in fact, addressing the larger matter of external motivation. Daniel Pink argued that such motivation is a type of stick or punishment and works for algorithmic tasks; unfortunately, the [2]**making** of friends and finding one's place in a social group is not really a task in which one can "follow a set of [3]**established*** instructions down a single pathway to one conclusion," which is how algorithmic activities succeed (Pink 15). Thus, this kind of [4]**debilitating** motivation led Blanco to further heartache with her hostile, cruel classmates. While the external motivation did not lead to success, when Blanco changed her perspective and her motivation became internal, she began to experience success as she realized that her negative experiences were actually a strength. Blanco realized that "I'm one of the lucky ones because I'm full of hope for the future" (245). Her new motivation was rather heuristic because she had to "experiment with possibilities and devise a novel solution" (Pink 16). It was this very change from the extrinsic to the intrinsic motivation that enabled her to overcome her past.

Answers Explained

1. This adjective form requires the present participle **enhancing**.
2. The gerund form requires the present participle **making**.
3. This adjective form requires the past participle **established**.
4. This adjective form requires the present participle **debilitating**.

Edit 9: Verbal Forms
find and fix the verb form errors

Elizabeth Deutsch Earle's essays, one written at 16 title "An Honest Doubter" and the other written 50 years later titled "Have I Learned Anything Important Since I was Sixteen?," offer interest insights into the way the passage of time affects belief. At 16, Earle grappled with a "blessings and a curse- a doubt, question mind" ("An Honest" 52). She was struggling to reconcile both the tenets of science and religion into her youthful philosophy. Her rule of the time was "to see what must be done and not do it, is a crime" (Earle "An Honest" 53). Fifty years later with a lifetime of experience to draw from, she has to some degree maintained her beliefs. Because as she puts it, "life is very often unfair," it can be difficult "to see what needs to be done and even harder actually to do it" (Earle "Have" 56-57). Nonetheless, she continues along the journey savoring life and try to make a difference. In comparing her writing after the passage of such time, it seems her personality core and desires are the same. Though I have not yet lived 50 years and so can't consider such an all encompass passage of time for my life, I can think about what I believed, wanted, and sought as a teenager compared to my current pursuits. I wish I had documented more of that young girl's hopes and dreams to evaluate whether she had achieved them. Regardless, feelings appreciative like Earle, I too realize that "I am happy right now" and I'm grateful for the life I have (Earle "Have" 57).

Edit 9: Suggested Answers

answers indicated in bold

Elizabeth Deutsch Earle's essays, one written at 16 [1]**titled**"An Honest Doubter" and the other written 50 years later titled "Have I Learned Anything Important Since I was Sixteen?", offer [2]**interesting** insights* into the way the passage of time affects* belief. At 16, Earle grappled with a "blessing and a curse - a [3]**doubting**, [4]**questioning** mind" (52). She was struggling to reconcile both the tenets of science and religion into her youthful philosophy. Her rule of the time was "to see what must be done and not do it, is a crime" (53). Fifty years later with a lifetime of experience to draw from, she has to some degree maintained her beliefs. Because as she puts it, "life is very often unfair," it can be difficult "to see what needs to be done and even harder actually to do it" (Earle 56-57). Nonetheless, she continues along the journey savoring life and trying to make a difference. In comparing her writing after the passage of such time, it seems the personality core and desires are the same. Though I have not yet lived 50 years and so can't consider such an all [5]**encompassing** passage of time for my life, I can think about what I believed, wanted, and sought as a teenager compared to my current pursuits. I wish I had documented* more of that young girl's hopes and dreams to evaluate whether she had achieved them. Regardless, [6]**feeling** appreciative like Earle, I too realize that "I am happy right now" and I'm grateful for the life I have (57).

Answers Explained

1. The adjective form requires the past participle **titled**.
2. This adjective form requires the present participle **interesting**.
3. This adjective form requires the present participle **doubting**.
4. This adjective form requires the present participle **questioning**.
5. This adjective form requires the present participle **encompassing**.
6. The gerund form requires the present participle **feeling**.

Edit 10: Verbal Forms
find and fix the verb form errors

Steve Porter, in "The 50-Percent Theory of Life," suggests an axiom to live by-- normal is a fluctuate circumstance. He argues, "Half the time things are better than normal; the other half, they are worse" (Porter 181). He provides a broad scale of life shape circumstances from the lowest point, the death of a love one, to the highest points, those moments of ultimate joy like marriage, childbirth, and doing dad-things with his son. Through his life, he has learned that while the awful, horrible circumstances do occur, they don't last forever; they are offset by all the proceeding and succeeding good circumstances of life. His belief that "worse than normal [won't] last for long" offers assurance to help him see hope in those bad times (Porter 182). This 50-Percent theory could be beneficial to those who have experienced difficulty, which is, honestly, most everyone, including me. I have had a rough couple of years losing several belove family members to that ultimate tragedy, death. These dark circumstances have certainly been at the bottom of my personal life scale; nonetheless, the pendulum is slowly and steadily swinging back to those bright moments that occur as well. It is helpful in those moments of darkness to remember that they will not last forever; nothing does. As Porter maintains, the positive experiences of my life can sustain me through these devastate dark times. Eventually, things will return back to normalcy where I live most of the time. I find the idea of the 50-Percent theory to be comforting in times of trouble.

Edit 10: Suggested Answers

answers indicated in bold

Steve Porter, in "The 50-Percent Theory of Life," suggests an axiom to live by-- normal is a [1]**fluctuating*** circumstance. He argues, "Half the time things are better than normal; the other half, they are worse" (Porter 181). He provides a broad scale of life [2]**shaping** circumstances from the lowest point, the death of a [3]**loved** one, to the highest points, those moments of ultimate joy like marriage, childbirth, and doing dad-things with his son. Through his life, he has learned that while the awful, horrible, circumstances do occur, they don't last forever; they are offset* by all the proceeding* and succeeding good circumstances of life. His belief that "worse than normal [won't] last for long" offers assurance* to help him see hope in those bad times (Porter 182). This 50-Percent theory* could be beneficial to those who have experienced difficulty, which is, honestly, most everyone, including me. I have had a rough couple* of years losing several [4]**beloved** family members to that ultimate tragedy, death. These dark circumstances have certainly been at the bottom of my personal life scale; nonetheless, the pendulum is slowly and steadily swinging back to those bright moments that occur as well. It is helpful in those moments of darkness to remember that they will not last forever; nothing does. As Porter maintains*, the positive experiences of my life can sustain* me through these [5]**devastating** dark times. Eventually*, things will return back to normalcy* where I live most of the time. I find the idea of the 50-Percent theory to be comforting in times of trouble.

Answers Explained

1. The adjective form requires the present participle **fluctuating**.
2. The adjective form requires the present participle **shaping**.
3. The adjective form requires the past participle **loved**.
4. The adjective form requires the past participle **beloved**.
5. The adjective form requires the present participle **devastating**.

SV AGREEMENT REVIEW

Grammar Review

5 Practice Edits

Knock the "t" off the "can't."

~ George Reeves

SV Agreement

Subject-verb agreement is required for all the present tenses and some past irregular tenses. Some aspects of subject-verb agreement are more problematic than others and will be briefly reviewed here.

Quickly review the examples below of both singular and plural subjects with their agreeing verb forms. The subjects are indicated in *italics* and the verb in **bold**.

Regular SV Agreement Examples

Academic Text

Students in college classes **write** many papers. *One* student **likes** writing while *another* **prefers** math. Nonetheless, *all* **have** to write well to succeed in college. Good *writing* **is** easy to read, and clear *ideas* **are** easy to understand. Not *everyone* **enjoys** writing, but the *skill* **needs** to be mastered anyway. *To learn to write* well **seems** to be a daunting task, but there **are** *techniques that* **make** it less overwhelming.

Singular Subjects with **Verbs**	Plural Subjects with **Verbs**
student **likes**	*students* **write**
another **prefers**	*all* **have**
writing **is**	*ideas* **are**
everyone **enjoys**	*techniques* **are**
skill **needs**	*that* **make**
to learn **seems**	

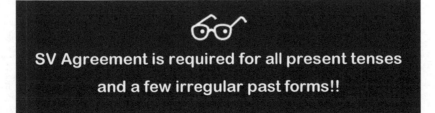

SV Agreement is required for all present tenses and a few irregular past forms!!

The simple present tense has a fundamental -S editing formula*. For the third person present, there is usually an -S, either on the verb with a singular subject or the noun with a plural subject.

3RD PERSON SINGULAR		3RD PERSON PLURAL	
noun	**verb + s**	noun + s	**verb**
student	**writes**	students	**write**

Therefore, an author* writes, a teacher instructs, and a student works hard, but authors write, teachers instruct, and students work hard.

Irregular verbs can create problems with subject-verb agreement, and three of the most commonly used verbs are the irregular auxiliary verbs be, have and do. Remember, the subjects are italicized, and the verbs are bolded in the example below.

Irregular SV Agreement Examples

Academic Text

As a writing instructor, *I* **am** very fond of grammar though my *students* **do** not always feel the same. *They* **have** difficulty with some of the verb forms. *Each* **is** specific in its requirements. Every *form* **does** not follow the exact same pattern. *They* **are** all important regardless. The *student* truly **has** to master all the patterns.

Singular Subjects with **Verbs**	*Plural Subjects* with **Verbs**
I **am**	*students* **do**
each **is**	*they* **have**
form **does**	*they* **are**
student **has.**	

CHART 8: IRREGULAR BE SV AGREEMENT

PAST		PRESENT	
I	**was**	I	**am**
You	**were**	You	**are**
He/she	**was**	He/she	**is**
We	**were**	We	**are**
They	**were**	They	**are**

Take a minute and review these vitally important forms in Chart 8: Irregular Be SV Agreement, and Chart 9: Have and Do SV Agreement.

CHART 9: HAVE AND DO SV AGREEMENT

SINGULAR		PLURAL	
noun	**has**	nouns	**have**
student	**does**	students	**do**

Look familiar? I'm sure you have previously spent a great deal of time with the information in these charts! The key to remember is that verbs, in the present tenses and a few irregular past tenses, require an added -S or -ES ending when used with third person singular nouns and pronouns!

This pattern also holds true with the complex present verb tenses like continuous, perfect, and perfect continuous as indicated in Chart 10.

CHART 10: COMPLEX PRESENT SUBJECT VERB AGREEMENT

PATTERN	STUDENT	STUDENTS
simple	**writes**	**write**
continuous	**is** writing	**are** writing
perfect	**has** written	**have** written
perfect continuous	**has** been writing	**have** been writing

With these complex tenses comprised* of a multiple-part verb form, it is the first auxiliary verb that takes the tense marker -S.

Nouns are fairly straightforward* in their number although some irregular nouns do also exist; thus, subject-verb agreement is relatively simple with nouns and verbs. However, with some pronouns, the agreement can be more tricky. The basic subjective pronouns of I, you, he, she, it, we, and they need little explanation. Nonetheless, other nouns and pronouns require a bit more review. Gerunds are almost always singular so should have a singular verb. Likewise*, the indefinite pronouns another, each, enough, less, little, much, one, and other are also always singular. Conversely*, the indefinite pronouns both, few, fewer, many, others, and several are always plural. With some effort, these forms can be simply memorized. Confusingly, some pronouns can be either singular or plural depending on the referent noun. These pronouns must not only be recognized but also must be evaluated carefully within the writing context to ensure* the correct SV Agreement.

> **Study Tip**
>
> Subject verb agreement is one of the easier verb forms to write correctly because it only requires recognizing the difference between one (singular) and more than one (plural). Take the time to check your subject-verb agreement forms! With a little effort, your mastery of this verb aspect can be excellent! You'll be glad you spend the time!

Chart 11 summarizes the subject-verb agreement requirements for the problem words which will be reviewed here.

CHART 11: OVERVIEW SV AGREEMENT PROBLEM WORDS

THESE WORDS CAN BE	SINGULAR	PLURAL
Gerunds	YES	NO
Infinitives	YES	NO
Indefinite PN: -body, -one, -thing	YES	NO
Indefinite PN: another, each, enough, less, little, much, one, other	YES	NO
Indefinite PN: both, few, fewer, many, others, several	NO	YES
Indefinite PN: all, any, more, most, some	YES	YES
Collective Noun	YES	YES
Relative Pronoun	YES	YES

Gerunds

Regarding SV Agreement, gerunds are easy to master because they are almost always singular. Thus, a gerund subject will almost always require a tense marker -S on the verb. The example sentences below italicize the gerund and bold the agreeing verb.

Gerund SV Agreement Examples

Writing **is** very time-consuming

Learning to edit verbs **was** instrumental in my writing improvement.

Editing **has been** the single most effective strategy I've learned.

Infinitives

Another kind of verbal is the infinitive (to + BF), which like a gerund can be used as a subject as in the sentence, "To write well gives much satisfaction." "To write" is the infinitive subject and "gives" is the singular agreeing verb form. Like the gerund, the infinitive subject is also always singular so requires a singular noun.

Infinitive SV Agreement Examples

To write well **is** a good goal* to have.

To learn **requires** a great deal of grit*

To edit my own work effectively **has become** a driving desire.

Gerund and infinitive subjects are always singular, so require a singular verb form!!

Indefinite Pronouns

Indefinite pronouns refer to nonspecific or general things. They can be singular, plural, or both. It is a good idea to either memorize or understand these indefinite pronouns because they are often used incorrectly for SV Agreement. Some indefinite pronouns, like those indicated the Chart 12 below, are always singular.

.

With these singular indefinite pronouns, when using a present verb pattern, you must always add the 3rd person tense marker -S.

CHART 12: BODY, ONE, AND THING

ALWAYS SINGULAR PRONOUNS	
anybody, anyone, anything	everybody, everyone, everything
nobody, no one, nothing	somebody, someone, something

Consider the following examples with these singular indefinite pronoun SV agreement examples.

Singular Indefinite Pronoun Examples

Does *anybody* know the homework?

Not *everybody* **loves** English.

Everything that I believe **has changed** with my education.

Someone **has forgotte**n to write his name on the test.

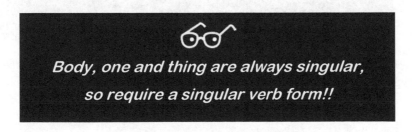

Body, one and thing are always singular,

so require a singular verb form!!

Additional singular Indefinite Pronouns are indicated in Chart 13.

ALWAYS SINGULAR PRONOUNS			
another	each	enough	less
little	much	one	other

Being singular, these indefinite pronouns will also take a singular tense marker -S for agreement.

More Indefinite Pronoun SV Agreement Examples

Another **is** required.	*Enough* **is** enough!
Little **was** said after the movie.	*One* **wants** to improve verb usage.
Each **states** a reason for being late.	*Less* **is** more.
Much **was** written by the teacher.	The *other* **is** lost.

Certain indefinite pronouns are always singular, so require a singular verb form!!

Some Indefinite Pronouns, like those indicated the Chart 14, are always plural.

PLURAL INDEFINITE PRONOUNS		
both	few	fewer
many	others	several

These plural indefinite pronouns are used in example sentences below.

Always Plural Indefinite Pronoun SV Agreement Examples

Both **are** acceptable.	*Others* **think** prepositions are hard to learn.
Many **need** to study more.	*Fewer* **think** verbs are the hardest.
Few **know** what he means.	*Several* of the teachers **are** here.

With these plural indefinite pronouns, the tense marker -S is never used.

Certain indefinite pronouns are always plural, so require a plural verb form!!

The indefinite pronouns, indicated in Chart 15, can be either singular or plural. Therefore, it is imperative to identify to which noun the pronoun refers to achieve agreement.

BOTH SINGULAR AND PLURAL				
all	any	more	most	some

Review the following examples of these indefinite pronouns.

Singular and Plural Indefinite Pronoun Examples

example	I need some *paper.* **Is** there *any* left?
explained	Singular *paper* makes *any* singular requiring singular irregular verb form **is**.
example	I can't find the *pencils.* **Are** there *any* over there?
explained	Plural *pencils* make *any* plural requiring plural irregular verb form **are**.
example	*Some* of the *book* **is** hard to understand.
explained	Singular *book* makes *some* singular requiring the singular irregular verb form **is**.
example	*Some* books **are** hard to understand.
explained	Plural *books* make *some* plural requiring the plural irregular verb form **are**.

With indefinite pronouns that can be both, you must identify* whether they are singular or plural. If singular, when using a present verb, you must always add the 3rd person tense marker -S.

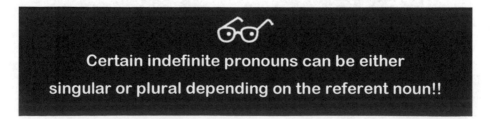

Certain indefinite pronouns can be either
singular or plural depending on the referent noun!!

Collective Nouns

Collective nouns can be highly confusing because they can be groups of things forming a single unit, thus requiring 3rd-person singular agreement, but they can also be individuals within the group acting independently, thus requiring 3rd-person plural agreement. Another consideration is the country origin of the English being used. For example, British English and American English often handle these instances differently; given the origin of this book, all rules herein are following the English academic standard. The key to using the correct agreement is deciding whether the noun is performing as a single unit or the noun is a group of individuals doing various actions separately.

Take a look at some common collective nouns in Chart 16 and their examples below.

CHART 16: COMMON COLLECTIVE NOUNS

POSSIBLY CONFUSING NOUNS			
audience	board	class	committee
company	department	faculty	family
group	society	school	team

Collective Noun SV Agreement Examples

example	The movie *audience* **laughs** at the funny scene.
explained	Singular as all members of the audience as a group laugh simultaneously.
example	Before the movie, the *audience* **turn** off their phones.
explained	Plural as audience members individually complete these actions.
example	The anxious *class* **worries** about the final exam.
explained	Singular as all members of the class as a group worry about the same test.
example	The *class* often **arrive** late.
explained	Plural as the individual students in the class arrive at various times.

Relative Pronouns

Relative pronouns begin relative clauses, also called adjective clauses. When used as a pronoun subject for the dependent clause, these pronouns modify* a noun, which can be either singular or plural. The relative pronoun mimics* the number used by the noun it modifies; hence, relative pronouns can be either singular or plural depending on the referent noun being used. Relative pronouns can modify all the noun roles of subjects, objects, or objects of prepositions.

Common relative pronouns are that, which, and who.

CHART 17: RELATIVE PRONOUNS

MOST COMMON		
Which	That	Who

As with some of the indefinite pronouns, relative pronouns always refer to something else in the sentence. It is imperative then to identify what referent noun the relative pronoun refers to for SV Agreement.

Relative Pronoun SV Agreement Examples

example	My *book that* **is** about Medical School Acceptance is available online.
explained	Singular *book* is the referent noun for singular relative pronoun *that* requiring the singular irregular verb form **is**.
example	Learning from *books, which* **are** topic specific, is a good study strategy.
explained	Plural *books* is the referent noun for plural relative pronoun *which* requiring the plural irregular verb form **are**.
example	It is important to a future *doctor, who* **wants** to attend medical* school.
explained	Singular *doctor* is the referent noun for singular relative pronoun *who* requiring the plural verb form **wants**.
example	It is important only to future *doctors, who* **want** to attend school.
explained	Plural *doctors* is the referent noun for plural relative pronoun *who* requiring the plural verb form **want**.

Irregular Adverbs

   Nouns, not adverbs like here and there, are generally used as sentence subjects. However, sometimes a sentence may be inverted✦ so that the adverbs "here" and "there" move to the beginning of the sentence looking like the noun subject. Take the sentence "The students are there." The plural noun "students" is clearly the sentence subject, and the plural verb form "are" agrees with it. If that sentence is inverted, it becomes "There are the students." In that case, even though the "there" has moved to the beginning of the sentence similar to a subject, it is actually not the subject. Actually, the subject is still the noun "students" just as it was before, but now it has been flipped. Therefore, to find SV Agreement in a sentence starting with the adverbs here or there, you must look to the object noun of the sentence to determine the number, not the adverb subject. This is an unusual sentence structure that requires special effort.

   Consider these example sentences below.

Irregular Adverb SV Agreement Examples

example	Here **is** the *teacher*.
explained	Singular *teacher* is the referent noun for singular irregular adverb here requiring singular irregular verb form **is**.
example	Here **are** my *books*.
explained	Plural *books* is the referent noun for plural irregular adverb here requiring plural irregular verb form **are**.
example	There **is** no *reason* for rudeness.
explained	Singular *reason* is the referent noun for singular irregular adverb there requiring the singular irregular verb form **is**.
example	There **are** the *students*.
explained	Plural *students* is the referent for plural irregular adverb here requiring the plural irregular verb form **are**.

> 👓
> Collective nouns, relative pronouns, and irregular adverbs
> can be singular or plural depending on the referent noun!!

Subject Verb Agreement Summary

- SV agreement requires the subject and verb to agree in person and number.
- Gerunds and infinitives should always use the singular verb form.
- Indefinite pronouns can be singular, plural, or both.
- For certain indefinite pronouns, the context decides the number for the singular or plural SV Agreement rule.
- Collective nouns can be either singular or plural depending on the context of a noun as a unit or as an individual.
- Relative pronouns modify nouns that can be either singular or plural depending on the noun being modified.
- Irregular adverb subjects can be either singular or plural depending on the referent noun object.

Study Tip

Though we are focused in this book on verbs, checking your verb agreement with the subject allows you to check your noun and article usage at the same time. This one verb focus allows you to check for three kinds of grammar errors! It can be very effective if performed efficiently.

SV Agreement Practice Edits

Here you will find five practice edits for subject-verb agreement with all verb patterns and with the special problem areas of gerunds, indefinite pronouns, collective nouns, relative pronouns, and irregular adverbs. You might try one of the Editing Strategies you haven't yet attempted, or you might just use your favorite thus far. Remember, you'll need to identify not just the main verb, but also the subject that accompanies that verb to correctly assess subject-verb agreement.

In the Answers Explained, you will find that changes have only been made to the incorrect verbs rather than the subjects; however, it may be possible to have changed the subjects too in your own editing. Don't assume your answer is incorrect just because it differs from the given answer!

Edit 11: SV Agreement
find and fix 5 verb form errors

Moreover, because today's society has such a soaring divorce rate, to live happily ever after are part of the fairytale appeal of the romance novel. Unfortunately, in the classic fairytale, it is always the unfortunate yet beautiful woman who get to marry the prince. Amanda Quick disregards the idea that the visibly, angelic woman should become royalty and enables the ordinary woman to become the princess and obtain the happy ending. In the novel *Seduction*, the heroine Sophy is described as not being "fashionably extreme in her coloring, being neither strikingly dark-haired nor angelically blond" and as being " no Grecian goddess" (Quick 5-6). Being an average looking woman prevent Sophy from being a paragon of beauty, yet it is she who marries the Earl of Ravenwood and becomes a Countess. Another heroine in the novel *Rendezvous* is not "beautiful…in the much-admired classical style" but in spite of her physical appearance, she too manage to marry an Earl and live happily ever after (Quick 19-20). Quick rejects the outdated belief that many has, which is that beauty is a requirement for the fairytale ending. At the same time, she supports the traditional idea that everlasting happiness is found through the institution of marriage.

Edit 11: Suggested Answers

answers indicated in bold

Moreover, because today's society has such a soaring divorce rate, to live happily ever after [1]**is** part of the fairytale appeal of the romance novel. Unfortunately, in the classic* fairytale, it is always the unfortunate yet beautiful woman who [2]**gets** to marry the prince. Amanda Quick disregards the idea that the visibly angelic woman should become royalty and enables the ordinary woman to become the princess and obtain* the happy ending. In the novel Seduction, the heroine Sophy is described as not being "fashionably extreme in her coloring, being neither strikingly dark-haired nor angelically blond" and as being "no Grecian goddess" (Quick 5-6). Being an average looking woman [3]**prevents** Sophy from being a paragon of beauty, yet it is she who marries the Earl of Ravenwood and becomes a Countess. Another heroine in the novel Rendezvous is not "beautiful… in the much-admired classical style" but in spite of her physical* appearance, she too [4]**manages** to marry an Earl and live happily ever after (Quick 19-20). Quick rejects the outdated belief that many [5]**have**, which is that beauty is a requirement for the fairytale ending. At the same time, she supports the traditional* idea that everlasting happiness is found through the institution of marriage.

Answers Explained

1. The singular infinitive *to live* requires the singular verb form **is**.
2. The singular referent noun *woman* requires the singular verb form **gets**.
3. The singular gerund *being* requires the singular verb form **prevents**.
4. The singular pronoun *she* requires the singular verb form **manages**.
5. The plural indefinite pronoun *many* requires the plural verb form **have**.

Edit 12: SV Agreement
find and fix 7 verb form errors

I enjoyed the article "Ten Ways to Think about Writing: Metaphoric Musings for College Writing Students." In this article, E. Shelley Reid offers three principles that basically sum up all the detailed writing rules of a class. In talking about these rules, I would like to start out of order with number three, which are "adapt to the audience and purpose [one is] writing for" (Reid 4). One that seem to be confusing for non-native students to understand are the audience; providing this understanding is imperative for a writing teacher like me to scaffold the assignment to meet the expectations of an educated audience. For example, in a college class, the audience expects appropriate MLA and other formatting conventions, expects a logical argument, expects detailed examples, and ultimately expects the paper to follow all the assigned guidelines given by the instructor. The audience need to be considered first of all; some of the onerous requisites that I require during a writing class falls under the category of understanding the audience. Thus, when the class think about these things, the students should not think that Prof. Undertree is just being strict and mean for no reason; in fact, there are always an academic reason for everything I do even if the student does not understand it.

Edit 12: Suggested Answers
answers indicated in bold

I enjoyed the article "Ten Ways to Think about Writing: Metaphoric Musings for College Writing Students." In this article, E. Shelley Reid offers three principles* that basically sum up all the detailed writing rules of a class. In talking about these rules, I would like to start out of order with number three, which [1]**is** "adapt to the audience and purpose [one is] writing for" (Reid 4). One that [3]**seems** to be confusing for non-native students to understand [2]**is** the audience; providing this understanding is imperative for a writing teacher like me to scaffold the assignment to meet the expectations of an educated audience. For example, in a college class, the audience expects appropriate MLA and other formatting conventions, expects a logical* argument, expects detailed examples, and ultimately expects the paper to follow all the assigned guidelines* given by the instructor. The audience [4]**needs** to be considered first of all; some of the onerous✧ requisites that I require during a writing class [5]**fall** under the category of understanding the audience. Thus, when the class [6]**thinks** about these things, the students should not think that Prof. Undertree is just being strict and mean for no reason; in fact, there [7]**is** always an academic reason for everything I do even if the student does not understand it.

Answers Explained

1. This singular referent noun *number* requires the singular verb form **is**.
2. The singular pronoun *one* requires the singular verb form **is**.
3. The plural referent noun *thing* requires the singular verb form **seems**.
4. The singular collective noun *audience* requires the singular verb form **needs**.
5. The plural indefinite pronoun *some* requires the plural verb form **fall**.
6. The singular collective noun *class* requires the singular verb form **thinks**.
7. The singular referent noun *reason* requires the singular verb form **is**.

Edit 13: SV Agreement
find and fix 5 verb form errors

Robert A. Heinlein has been an influence on my own views since I grew up reading his science fiction work. However, his views in "Our Noble, Essential Decency" is even more relevant than all his fictional stories combined. No stranger to society's problems like crime, corruption, and even war, he still makes a case for the goodness of mankind, being "proud to be a human being" (Heinlein 121). Heinlein believes in the "honesty, courage, intelligence, durability, and goodness" of humankind – "yellow, white, black, red, [and] brown" (121). Personally, Heinlein's belief in mankind's "honesty, insatiable curiosity, unlimited courage and noble essential decency" are comforting today in the wake of the deadliest mass shooting in American history that occurred this week (121). Terrible things occur daily so that everyone worry about the future, but the good people of the world do still rise and stand for decency, helping others in the face of tragedy. It is so easy to fall prey to the negative thoughts and stereotypes swirling around today, especially for anyone who find others suspicious or even evil. Instead, I would rather look for the stories of good behavior. People all around the world, and in America itself, are reaching out to others, assisting in both small and large ways every day, all day long. I want to be one of those people, someone who expect the best, not the worst of others. I want to believe, like Heinlein, that people will "always make it, survive, endure" (121).

Edit 13: Suggested Answers

answers indicated in bold

Robert A. Heinlein has been an influence on my own views since I grew up reading his science fiction work. However, his views in "Our Noble, Essential Decency" [1]**are** even more relevant than all his fictional stories combined. No stranger to society's problems like crime, corruption, and even war, he still makes a case for the goodness of mankind, being "proud to be a human being" (Heinlein 121). Heinlein believes in the "honesty, courage, intelligence*, durability, and goodness" of humankind – "yellow, white, black, red, [and] brown" (121). Personally, Heinlein's belief in mankind's "honesty, insatiable curiosity, unlimited courage and noble essential decency" [2]**is** comforting today in the wake of the deadliest mass shooting in American history that occurred this week (121). Terrible things occur daily so that everyone [3]**worries** about the future, but the good people of the world do still rise and stand for decency, helping others in the face of tragedy. It is so easy to fall prey to the negative thoughts and stereotypes swirling around today, especially for anyone who [4]**finds** others suspicious or even evil. Instead, I would rather look for the stories of good behavior. People all around the world, and in America itself, are reaching out to others, assisting* in both small and large ways every day, all day long. I want to be one of those people, someone who [5]**expects** the best, not the worst in others. I want to believe, like Heinlein, that people will "always make it, survive*, endure" (121).

Answers Explained

1. The plural noun *views* requires the plural verb form **are**.
2. The singular noun *belief* requires the singular verb form **is**.
3. The singular indefinite pronoun *everyone* requires the singular verb form **worries**.
4. The singular referent noun *anyone* requires the singular verb form **finds**.
5. The singular referent noun *someone* requires the singular verb form **expects**.

Edit 14: SV Agreement
find and fix the verb form errors

In the short story "Thank You Ma'am," Langston Hughes tell the story of a young man whose life may be changed by a brief encounter with a strong woman. Roger is a neglected teenager about fourteen or fifteen years old, who have no one at home to care for him or teach him right from wrong. Society seem to have forgotten about him. Wanting a pair of fancy shoes cause him to attempt to snatch the purse of a formidable woman, Mrs. Luella Bates Washington Jones. Unfortunately for Roger, Mrs. Jones is stronger and more prepared than he so that his trying to grab her bag enable his own capture in her grasp. Mrs. Jones both physically and verbally chastises Roger, and then drags him off to her house to feed him, lecture him, offer him trust, and ultimately give him the money for the very shoes he wanted. Needless to say, her kindness offer a glimmer of previously unthought-of choices. However, there are nothing Mrs. Jones asks for, not even thanks, and sends the boy on his way. In the story, Hughes suggests that Roger can change because of Mrs. Jones' actions. At the beginning of the story, Roger roams the streets late at night, only worrying about his desires, but once Mrs. Jones shows him the tiniest bit of kindness, he does "not want to be mistrusted now" (19). Moreover, for perhaps the first time in life, he wants to give someone thanks, but he does not know how. Through this story, Hughes shows how small acts could have huge consequences.

Edit 14: Suggested Answers

answers indicated in bold

In the short story "Thank You Ma'am," Langston Hughes [1]**tells** the story of a young man whose life may be changed by a brief encounter with a strong woman. Roger is a neglected teenager about fourteen or fifteen years old, who [2]**has** no one at home to care for him or teach him right from wrong. Society [3]**seems** to have forgotten about him. Wanting a pair of fancy shoes [4]**causes** him to attempt to snatch the purse of a formidable woman, Mrs. Luella Bates Washington Jones. Unfortunately for Roger, Mrs. Jones is stronger and more prepared than he so that his trying to grab her bag [5]**enables** his own capture in her grasp. Mrs. Jones both physically and verbally chastises Roger, and then drags him off to her house to feed him, lecture* him, offer him trust, and ultimately give him the money for the very shoes he wanted. Needless to say, her kindness [6]**offers** a glimmer of previously unthought-of choices. However, there [7]**is** nothing Mrs. Jones asks for, not even thanks, and sends the boy on his way. In the story, Hughes suggests that Roger can change because of Mrs. Jones' actions. At the beginning of the story, Roger roams the streets late at night, only worrying about his desires, but once Mrs. Jones shows him the tiniest bit of kindness, he does "not want to be mistrusted now" (19). Moreover, for perhaps the first time in life, he wants to give someone thanks, but he does not know how. Through this story, Hughes shows how small acts could have huge consequences.

Answers Explained

1. The singular noun *Hughes* requires the singular verb form **tells**.
2. The singular referent noun *teenager* requires the singular verb form **has**.
3. The singular collective noun *society* requires the singular verb form **seems**.
4. The singular gerund *wanting* requires the singular verb form **causes**.
5. The singular gerund requires the singular verb form **enables**.
6. The singular noun *kindness* requires the singular verb form **offers**.
7. The singular referent noun *nothing* requires the singular verb form **is**.

Edit 15: SV Agreement
find and fix the verb form errors

"The Quickening" by Lisa Interollo shows how Vicky, a young shoplifter, started her life of crime and reaped the consequences of her actions. Offering a glimpse into the possibility of Vicky's change provide inspiration for others in similar circumstances. Vicky has parents who love her and try to do the best by her, but they are not very aware of her actions. Her older sister teaches Vicky the excitement of shoplifting when she is little, and after that, to shoplift give Vicky a "quickening" or thrill. When her mother discovers Vicky's actions, she is embarrassed but does not punish the girl. Clearly, her mother is not fulfilling her responsibilities to the children. Vicky is not poor, and she does not steal from hunger, but do so from boredom and anger. This is shown when she and her friends steal Gouda cheeses from the delicatessen and do not even eat them, but just throw them into the park. Vicky says that Susan and she "recognizes every feeling- and every gradation of every feeling- that arises in the process of taking something" (Interollo 41). Eventually, a teacher named Mr. Donnelly helps Vicky see a better way. He expresses his displeasure at her actions and tells her "I wish you'd cut it out … I would hate to see you screw things up for yourself" (Interollo 46). Telling her that she is smart and has enough guts to find a better way encourage Vicky to find that "the wanting is gone" (Interollo 47). Interello suggests that it was the desire to be recognized that caused Vicky's theft, and once she had that from Mr. Donnelly, she was able to stop.

Edit 15: Suggested Answers

answers indicated in bold

"The Quickening" by Lisa Interollo shows how Vicky, a young shoplifter, started her life of crime and reaped the consequences of her actions. Offering a glimpse into the possibility of Vicky's change [1]**provides** inspiration for others in similar circumstances. Vicky has parents who love her and try to do the best by her, but they are not very aware of her actions. Her older sister teaches Vicky the excitement of shoplifting when she is little, and after that, to shoplift [2]**gives** Vicky a "quickening" or thrill. When her mother discovers Vicky's actions, she is embarrassed but does not punish the girl. Clearly, her mother is not fulfilling her responsibilities to the children. Vicky is not poor, and she does not steal from hunger but [3]**does** so from boredom and anger. This is shown when she and her friends steal Gouda cheeses from the delicatessen and do not even eat them, but just throw them into the park. Vicky says that Susan and she "[4]**recognize** every feeling- and every gradation of every feeling- that arises in the process of taking something" (Interollo 41). Eventually, a teacher named Mr. Donnelly helps Vicky see a better way. He expresses his displeasure at her actions and tells her "I wish you'd cut it out … I would hate to see you screw things up for yourself" (Interollo 46). Telling her that she is smart and has enough guts to find a better way [5]**encourages** Vicky to find that "the wanting is gone" (Interollo 47). Interello suggests that it was the desire to be recognized that caused Vicky's theft, and once she had that from Mr. Donnelly, she was able to stop.

Answers Explained

1. The singular gerund *offering* requires the singular verb form **provides**.
2. The singular infinitive *to shoplift* requires the singular verb form **gives**.
3. The singular pronoun *she* requires the singular verb form **does**.
4. The plural noun *Susan* and pronoun *she* requires the plural verb form **recognize**.
5. The singular gerund *telling* requires the singular verb form **encourages**.

6

TENSE PATTERN REVIEW

Grammar Review

5 Practice Edits

Little by little does the trick.

~Aesope

Tense Pattern Verb Forms

The main verbs in English have multiple forms of expression and accompanying* rules. Every verb in English has three times (telling when for past, present, and future) and four aspects (telling how in simple, continuous, perfect, and perfect continuous) for a total of twelve basic forms to express meaning. There are also two English voices: active voice (AV) and passive voice (PV), for a total of twenty-four patterns to form each English verb. Specific forms are required for each pattern, so eliminating obligatory* word endings or substituting* erroneous endings causes verb form errors. Common errors in the verb form patterns occur with the present participle and the past participle of the verb. These verb tense patterns are not complicated but must be used correctly. In academic writing, a paragraph may move through multiple tense patterns.

Consider the example paragraph below with the verb patterns numbered in each sentence.

Tense Pattern Examples

Academic Text

Grammar rules [1]**are** often **taught** in school. I [2]**enjoy** studying grammar because I [3]**have seen** what a benefit quality writing [4]**can bring**. Editing practice [5]**will enable** writing improvement. My class [6]**is working** to improve its editing skills. They [7]**have been studying** all semester. They [8]**have improved** so much. Their mastery of the verbs [9]**should be completed** by the end of the semester, and I [10]**will be** so proud!

Tense Patterns Defined

1. Simple Present PV: **are taught**
2. Simple Present AV: **enjoy**
3. Present Perfect AV: **have seen**
4. Modal Simple AV: **can bring**
5. Simple Future AV: **will enable**

6. Present Continuous AV: **is working**
7. Present Perfect Continuous AV: **have been studying**
8. Present Perfect AV: **have improved**
9. Modal Simple PV: **should be completed**
10. Simple Future: **will be**

While this lesson will not cover the function or usage of the various tenses since the focus here is only verb form, it is necessary to briefly explain the differences between the voices as they each have their own verb form patterns.

Study Tip

Verb form patterns are rather like puzzle pieces in that they go together in certain ways and changing one piece for another creates a different picture. It is worth the time and effort to memorize these patterns; they don't change. They are the foundation of all sentences. If you can immediately recognize whether a verb is in active or passive voice because of its included components or you can immediately recognize that a present or past participle is missing, then you will be far on the road to verb mastery!

Active Voice

In the Active Voice (AV), a noun sentence subject completes an action with a verb to or for a noun direct object. For example, in the sentence " Prof. Undertree writes a book," "Prof. Undertree" is the noun subject completing the verb action "writes" of the noun direct object "a book." Each of the 12 verb patterns for AV has specific pattern requirements that must be followed unceasingly✣.

If you have not yet memorized these patterns in Chart 18, now would be a good time to do so.

CHART 18: OVERVIEW VERB FORM AV PATTERNS

TENSE		PAST	PRESENT	FUTURE
SIMPLE	FORMULA	BF + ED Irregular Varies	BF 3rd Singular +S	FTR + BF
	EXAMPLE	edited wrote	edit edits	will edit
CONTINUOUS	FORMULA	PST BE + PRS PART	PRS BE + PRS PART	FTR BE + PRS PAR
	EXAMPLE	was editing were editing	am editing is editing are editing	will be editing
PERFECT	FORMULA	PST HAVE + PST PART	PRS HAVE + PST PART	FTR HAVE + PST PART
	EXAMPLE	had edited had written	have edited have written	will have edited will have written
PERFECT CONTINUOUS	FORMULA	PST HAVE + PST PART BE + PRS PART	PRS HAVE + PST PART BE + PRS PART	FTR HAVE + PST PART BE +PRS PART
	EXAMPLE	had been editing	have been editing has been editing	will have been editing

Passive Voice

In the passive voice (PV), the noun subject and the noun object switch positions in the sentence causing the verb form to also change. Look at the sentence, "A book is written by Prof. Undertree." The "book" noun object is receiving the verb action "is written" by the noun subject "Prof. Undertree." There are also 12 forms of PV, each with its own rules of formation; however, not all 12 forms are used equally in academic writing. The forms of future continuous and perfect, and past/present/future perfect continuous are rarely used, so will not be reviewed here.

The most common PV patterns with examples are indicated in Chart 19 below.

CHART 19: OVERVIEW VERB FORM PV PATTERNS

TENSE		PAST	PRESENT	FUTURE
SIMPLE	FORMULA	PST BE + PST PART	PRS BE + PST PART	FTR BE + PST PART
	EXAMPLE	was / were edited	am / is / are edited	will be edited
CONTINUOUS	FORMULA	PST BE + PRS PART BE +PRS PART	PRS BE + PRS PART BE +PRS PART	
	EXAMPLE	was / were being edited	am / is / are being edited	
PERFECT	FORMULA	PST HAVE + PST PART BE +PST PART	PRS HAVE + PST PART BE +PST PART	
	EXAMPLE	had been edited	have / has been edited	

Modals

Modals are a sub-class of auxiliary verbs that specify* meaning for the main verb and are used to create various functions like obligation and condition. They allow the meaning of verbs to be mitigated* and provide for polite address. The modal itself never takes a tense marker and combines with the base form verb. Modals can be used with all the tenses. With the simple form, the base form main verb is used. With the more complex forms of continuous, perfect, and perfect continuous, the auxiliary base form verb is used, but the other patterns do not change.

English has nine basic modals: can, could, may, might, must, shall, should, will and would. The modal pattern with the various tense patterns and examples is indicated in Chart 20.

CHART 20: OVERVIEW MODAL MAIN VERB FORMS AND VOICE PATTERNS

TENSE		AV	PV
SIMPLE	FORMULA	MDL + BF	MDL + BE + PST PART
	EXAMPLE	can edit	must be edited
CONTINUOUS	FORMULA	MDL + BE + PRS PART	MDL+ BE + PRS PART BE + PST PART
	EXAMPLE	could be editing	should be being edited
PERFECT	FORMULA	MDL+ HAVE + PST PART	MDL + HAVE + PST PART BE + PST PART
	EXAMPLE	may have edited	would have been edited
PERFECT CONTINUOUS	FORMULA	MDL + HAVE + PST PART BE + PRS PART	
	EXAMPLE	might have been editing	

Study Tip

Ought to, have to, had better, and need to are more complex phrases sometimes used as modals as well. Each of these phrases is also followed by the base form of the verb. Consider the following examples:

Students ought to edit their work.

They have to edit their verb forms.

Everybody had better edit more carefully.

Everybody needs to learn to edit better!

There are two basic kinds of verb pattern form errors. The first is using an incorrect ending or omitting the ending on one of the pattern pieces; the other is omitting one or more of the required pattern pieces. With an increase in verb pattern elements*, there is more opportunity to omit* required endings or insert incorrect endings; therefore, it is important to double check each form in the pattern.

Incorrect Endings

Review the examples below with incorrect and revised* AV verb pattern usage.

AV Verb Pattern Error Examples

error	I **am wrote** a chapter* about verb form.
explained	The present participle verb form **writing** is required in this AV present continuous pattern. *(PRS BE + PRS PART)*
revised	I **am writing** a chapter about verb form.
error	They **have write** many essays for class.
explained	The past participle verb form **written** is required in this AV present perfect pattern. *(PRS HAVE + PST PART)*
revised	They **have written** many essays for class.
error	You **will have be practice** your writing a lot by the end of the semester.
explained	The past participle verb form **been** and the present participle verb form **practicing** is required in this AV future perfect continuous pattern. *(FTR HAVE + PST PART BE + PRS PART)*
revised	You **will have been practicing** your writing a lot by the end of the semester.

Every tense pattern in Active Voice has its own required pattern formation!!

Review the examples below with incorrect and revised PV form usage.

PV Verb Pattern Error Examples

error	The exercises **were implement** by the students.
explained	The past participle verb form **implemented** is required in this PV past simple verb pattern. (PST BE + PST PART)
revised	The exercises **were implemented*** by the students.
error	Great care with verbs **is be taken** by the students.
explained	The present participle **being** is required in this PV present continuous verb pattern. *(PRS BE + PRS PART BE + PST PART)*
revised	Great care with verbs **is being taken** by the students.
error	Books **have be made** available in the library.
explained	The past participle verb form **been** is required in this PV present perfect continuous verb pattern. *(PRS HAVE + PST PART BE + PST PART)*
revised	Books **have been made** available in the library.

Every tense pattern in Passive Voice has its own required pattern formation!!

Review the examples below of correct and incorrect modals with main verb forms.

Modal Verb Pattern Error Examples

error	One who **can writes** well may be more successful than other students.
explained	The base verb form **write** is required in this AV modal simple verb pattern. *(MDL +BF)*
revised	One who **can write** well may be more successful than other students.
error	I **might have be writing** all night long had I not been so exhausted.
explained	The past participle verb form **been** is required in this AV modal perfect continuous verb pattern. *(MDL + HAVE + PST PART BE +PRS PART)*
revised	I **might have been writing** all night long had I not been so exhausted.
error	The paper **should has been written** yesterday.
explained	The base verb form **have** is required in this PV modal perfect verb pattern. *(MDL + HAVE + PST PART BE + PST PART)*
revised	The paper **should have been written** yesterday.

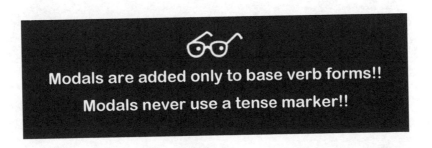

Modals are added only to base verb forms!!
Modals never use a tense marker!!

Omitted Patterns Pieces

Each aspect of the verb pattern is required for each pattern. It is not allowed, for instance, to omit the "be" if using the continuous form or the "been" if using the perfect continuous form. Make sure to double check your verb tense patterns so that all the pieces are included*.

Review the examples below of omitting required aspects of the verb tense patterns.

Missing Pattern Pieces Error Examples

error	Because of the weather today, he **going** to get to school late.
explained	The auxiliary verb **is** is required in this AV progressive verb pattern. *(PRS BE + PRS PART)*
revised	Because of the weather today, he **is going** to get to school late.
error	I've looked all over but the book **gone** from the desk.
explained	The auxiliary verb **is** is required in this PV simple verb pattern. *(PRS BE + PST PART)*
revised	I've looked all over, but the book **is gone** from the desk.
error	The final exams **have graded** by Prof. Undertree.
explained	The past participle **been** is required for the PV present perfect verb form pattern. *(PRS HAVE +PST PART BE+ PST PART)*
revised	The final exams **have been graded** by Prof. Undertree.

Notice with the following examples, there are alternative* meanings for these sentences. That is one of the reasons it is imperative to use your verb forms correctly. Not only do verb errors show poor language usage, even more importantly, they cause the sentence meaning to be confusing.

Make sure that all the parts of the verb being used are formed correctly!

Multiple Meaning Error Examples

error	She **has taking** her work more seriously this year.
explained	The present participle verb form **taken** is required in this AV present perfect verb form pattern. *(PRS HAVE + PST PART)* The past participle verb form **been** is required in this AV present perfect continuous verb form pattern. *(PRS HAVE + PST PART BE + PRS PART)*
revised	She **has taken** her work more seriously this year. She **has been taking** her work more seriously this year.
error	The class is edit the essays today.
explained	The present participle verb form **editing** is required in this AV present continuous verb form pattern. *(PRS BE + PRS PART)* The present verb form **has** is required in this AV present perfect verb form pattern. *(PRS HAVE + PST PART)*
revised	The class **is editing** the essays today. The class **has edited** the essays today.

As you can see, the patterns increase in complexity from simple to perfect continuous. In the formation of these patterns, it is imperative* to have the correct ending for the various tenses, or they simply don't make any sense to the reader.

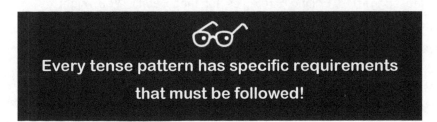

Every tense pattern has specific requirements that must be followed!

Tense Pattern Summary

- A combination of modals, base forms, present participles and past participles make up the verb tense patterns.

- The correct form must be used appropriately for each verb tense pattern.

- Each AV pattern and PV pattern has required verb forms.

- Modals never take a tense marker.

- Modals add to base form of main or auxiliary verb in the AV and PV patterns.

- Each of the forms requires specific endings.

- Using the wrong ending creates an error.

- Omitting verb endings creates an error.

- Omitting required pattern pieces creates an error.

Study Tip

Learn the verb tense patterns. Recognize them in your own writing! Noticing these patterns is really easy to do if you take time and edit carefully! Your writing will improve so much when you master these forms! I promise!

Tense Pattern Practice Edits

Here you will find five practice edits with missing or incorrect endings in the verb forms. Try one of the suggested Editing Strategies for these edits. You might try the strategy of reading aloud here. If you use isolation of errors, make sure that you consider all the verbs in the sentence. Upon completion of the edits, don't forget to check your answers too!

Edit 16: Main Verb Patterns
find and fix 5 verb form errors

Motivation was a definite factor in Michael Oher's ultimate success. Being homeless, he was live on the charity of others, which undoubtedly caused him to want to change his circumstances as he sought to please everyone with his appearance and manners to fit in. He explained how he "tried to do [his] best, was respectful of the house where [he]was stay, and presented the best face [he] coulds" present by staying clean-shaven and always ironing his clothes (Oher and Yaeger 133). Oher was, in fact, addressing the larger matter of external motivation as he was concern with what others thought of his appearance. Such motivation is a type of stick or punishment and works for algorithmic tasks, in which one can "follow a set of established instructions down a single pathway to one conclusion," which is how algorithmic activities succeed (Pink 15). In this case, meeting a specific expected dress standard helped Oher fit in and come to the attention of Tuohy family who ultimately adopted him. The Tuohy's modeled personal ambition for Oher enabling him to internalize a new motivation for success. Oher reports that "I was try to open doors and they were trying to show me the way through. It would never have worked if it had been one-sided: just me pushing…or just them guiding" (139). It was a combination of extrinsic motivation through the effort of the Tuohys and the intrinsic motivation in his own responsibilities that enabled him to succeed.

Edit 16: Suggested Answers
answers indicated in bold

Motivation was a definite factor in Michael Oher's ultimate success. Being homeless, he [1]**was living** on the charity of others, which undoubtedly caused him to want to change his circumstances as he sought to please everyone with his appearance and manners to fit in. He explained how he "tried to do [his] best, was respectful of the house where [he] [2]**was staying**, and presented the best face [he] [3]**could**" **present** by staying clean-shaven and always ironing his clothes (Oher and Yaeger 133). Oher was, in fact, addressing the larger matter of external motivation as he [4]**was concerned** with what others thought of his appearance. Such motivation is a type of stick or punishment and works for algorithmic tasks, in which one can "follow a set of established instructions down a single pathway to one conclusion," which is how algorithmic activities succeed (Pink 15). In this case, meeting a specific expected dress standard helped Oher fit in and come to the attention of Tuohy family who ultimately adopted him. The Tuohy's modeled personal ambition for Oher enabling him to internalize a new motivation for success. Oher reports that "I [5]**was trying** to open doors and they were trying to show me the way through. It would never have worked if it had been one-sided: just me pushing…or just them guiding" (139). It was a combination of extrinsic motivation through the effort of the Tuohys and the intrinsic motivation in his own responsibilities that enabled him to succeed.

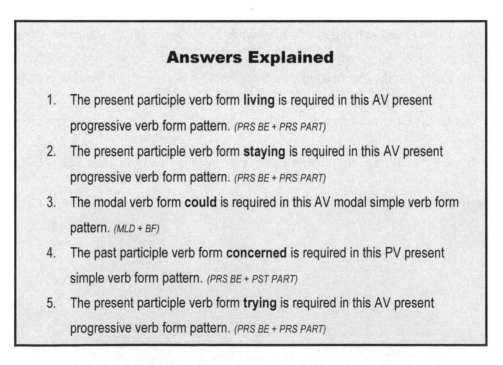

Answers Explained

1. The present participle verb form **living** is required in this AV present progressive verb form pattern. *(PRS BE + PRS PART)*
2. The present participle verb form **staying** is required in this AV present progressive verb form pattern. *(PRS BE + PRS PART)*
3. The modal verb form **could** is required in this AV modal simple verb form pattern. *(MLD + BF)*
4. The past participle verb form **concerned** is required in this PV present simple verb form pattern. *(PRS BE + PST PART)*
5. The present participle verb form **trying** is required in this AV present progressive verb form pattern. *(PRS BE + PRS PART)*

Edit 17: Main Verb Patterns
find and fix 4 verb form errors

1692 was a dark year for justice in American History. From February through September of 1692 in Salem Village, Massachusetts hundreds of men, women, and children accused of witchcraft. Many of the accused suffered the loss of their liberty, and often spent the remainder of their lives in prison awaiting trial. They also lost lands and livelihoods while they languished in prison. Age was not a consideration for the accused as the youngest was a 4-year-old child named Dorcas Good (Hill). Those of the accused who confessed to the crimes of witchcraft found guilty and then most often turned into the accusers themselves. None who confessed were executed. The examinations were stopped before many of the accused actually tried for the crime of witchcraft. Of those convicted of the crime of witchcraft, nineteen men and women were hang, four men and women died in prison, and one man was pressed to death between heavy stones (Breslaw). One of the executed women was a seventy-year-old grandmother named Rebecca Nurse.

Edit 17: Suggested Answers

answers indicated in bold

1692 was a dark year for justice in American History. From February through September of 1692 in Salem Village, Massachusetts hundreds of men, women, and children [1]**were accused** of witchcraft. Many of the accused suffered the loss of their liberty, and often spent the remainder of their lives in prison awaiting trial. They also lost lands and livelihoods while they languished in prison. Age was not a consideration for the accused as the youngest was a 4-year-old child named Dorcas Good (Hill). Those of the accused who confessed to the crimes of witchcraft [2]**were found** guilty and then most often turned into the accusers themselves. None who confessed were executed. The examinations were stopped before many of the accused [3]**were** actually **tried** for the crime of witchcraft. Of those convicted of the crime of witchcraft, nineteen men and women were [4]**hung**, four men and women died in prison, and one man was pressed to death between heavy stones (Breslaw). One of the executed women was a seventy-year-old grandmother named Rebecca Nurse.

Answers Explained

1. The plural past irregular verb form **were** is required in this PV past simple verb form pattern. *(PST BE + PST PART)*

2. The plural past irregular verb form **were** is required in this PV past simple verb form pattern. *(PST BE + PST PART)*

3. The plural past irregular verb form **were** is required in this PV past simple verb form pattern. *(PST BE + PST PART)*

4. The irregular past participle verb form **hung** is required in this PV past simple verb form pattern. *(PST BE + PST PART)*

Edit 18: Main Verb Patterns
find and fix 2 verb form errors

Phyllis Allen, in "Leaving Identity Issues to Other Folks," elucidates her beliefs about personal identity. She announces that her identity has change over the course of her life while providing detailed examples of the eras she lived through as a black woman, beginning with the sixties, moving through the seventies, eighties, and nineties, and ending in the new millennium. Through her fantastic journey, she learned that she is "free to be whoever [she] choose[s] to be" (Allen 12). Driving this fundamental belief is the idea that she should be the best she can be in whatever she endeavors. Like Allen, I hold the similar axiom to do the best I can in my life. While Allen focuses here on personal identity being shaped by the culture and period she has live in, I relate more to the idea of work greatly shaping my identity. For me, my job as an instructor is an integral part of my identity; I can't imagine myself without my teaching. Not only do I physically go to work and teach, but I also mentally prepare current lessons and future lessons without ceasing. This very paragraph is an example of my teaching at work. I am not only my profession, of course. Educating and helping others master language while facilitating their writing development are parts of the best of me. I, like Allen, seek to "be the best I can be" and help others in achieving the same goal (10).

Edit 18: Suggested Answers

answers indicated in bold

Phyllis Allen, in "Leaving Identity Issues to Other Folks," elucidates* her beliefs about personal identity. She announces that her identity [1]**has changed** over the course of her life while providing detailed examples of the eras she lived through as a black woman, beginning with the sixties, moving through the seventies, eighties, and nineties, and ending in the new millennium. Through her fantastic journey, she learned that she is "free to be whoever [she] choose[s] to be" (Allen 12). Driving this fundamental belief is the idea that she should be the best she can be in whatever she endeavors. Like Allen, I hold the similar axiom to do the best I can in my life. While Allen focuses here on personal identity being shaped by the culture and period* she [2]**has lived** in, I relate more to the idea of work greatly shaping my identity. For me, my job as an instructor is an integral part of my identity; I can't imagine myself without my teaching. Not only do I physically go to work and teach, but I also mentally* prepare current lessons and future lessons without ceasing. This very paragraph is an example of my teaching at work. I am not only my profession, of course. Educating and helping others master language while facilitating their writing development are parts of the best of me. I, like Allen, seek to "be the best I can be" and help others in achieving the same goal (10).

Answers Explained

1. The past participle verb form **changed** is required in this AV present perfect verb form pattern. *(PRS HAVE + PST PART)*

2. The past participle verb form **lived** is required in this AV present perfect verb form pattern. *(PRS HAVE + PST PART)*

Edit 19: Main Verb Patterns
find and fix the verb form errors

Very young children learn best through tactile and kinetic teaching, and classrooms usually reflect such learning styles. As children matriculate, tactile and kinetic methods are gradually decrease, and visual and auditory teaching methods gradually increased until the fifth-grade, and sixth-grade classrooms primarily use visual and auditory teaching methods according to Joy M. Reid. For the rest of an American student's scholastic career, information is mostly given orally through lectures or explanations. Questions are ask as part of the learning process. Value placed on the written demonstration of ideas, techniques, and solutions. Whether or not students learn most effectively with these types of methods has be largely irrelevant. Many of the current classroom teaching techniques give little consideration to the learning style differences or only consider the preferences of mainstream English speakers. Students have have to adapt to the visual-auditory-based American educational system.

Edit 19: Suggested Answers
answers indicated in bold

Very young children learn best through tactile and kinetic teaching, and classrooms usually reflect such learning styles. As children matriculate, tactile and kinetic methods [1]**are** gradually **decreased**, and visual and auditory teaching methods [2]**are** gradually **increased** until the fifth grade*, and sixth-grade classrooms primarily use visual and auditory teaching methods according to Joy M. Reid. For the rest of an American student's scholastic career, information is mostly given orally through lectures or explanations. Questions [3]**are asked** as part of the learning process. Value [4]**is placed** on the written demonstration of ideas, techniques, and solutions. Whether or not students learn most effectively with these types of methods [5]**has been** largely irrelevant. Many of the current classroom teaching techniques give little consideration to the learning style differences or only consider the preferences of mainstream English speakers. Students [6]**have had** to adapt* to the visual-auditory-based American educational system.

Answers Explained

1. The past participle verb form **decreased** is required in this PV present simple verb form pattern.*(PRS BE + PST PART)*
2. The plural present irregular verb form **are** is required in this PV present simple verb form pattern. *(PRS BE + PST PART)*
3. The past participle verb form **asked** is required in this PV present simple verb form pattern. *(PRS BE + PST PART)*
4. The singular present irregular verb form **is** is required in this PV present simple verb form pattern. *(PRS BE + PST PART)*
5. The irregular past participle verb form **been** is required in this AV modal perfect verb form pattern. *(MDL HAVE + PST PART)*
6. The irregular past participle verb form **had** is required in this AV present perfect verb form pattern. *(PRS HAVE + PST PART)*

Edit 20: Main Verb Patterns
find and fix the verb form errors

In trying to create a new American language, Noah Webster was unable to change English phonology and morphology to the degree he wished (Shoemaker). Nevertheless, there is no doubt his spelling book was a dominant force in the development of the country's awareness of language. Very few other textbooks have ever produce the kind of unifying force initiated by Webster. The strong influence of the Blue-Back speller cannot be pins on any one factor. The book was uniquely American, and it was the first of its kind. It filled a void in the national consciousness, which provided a sense of unity within the entire population. The book linked the schoolhouse with the community. Moreover, it connected the poorest child with the highest office in the land, the president of the United States. Furthermore, the book provided longevity for a new and beginning nation as it was the standard for over one hundred years. Though the changes to the actual English language were few, this small American speller commenced a literary unification of the country's language that still exists today The days are long over that America could be mocks for its lack of language and literature. Now, countless students from around the world come to the United States to learn English and obtain degrees from American Universities. America's language still called English and not all that different from England's English, yet there shoulds be no doubt that Americans have a strong sense of linguistic nationalism.

Edit 20: Suggested Answers
answers indicated in bold

In trying to create a new American language, Noah Webster was unable to change English phonology and morphology to the degree he wished. Nevertheless, there is no doubt his spelling book was a dominant force in the development of the country's awareness of language. Very few other textbooks [1]**have** ever **produced** the kind of unifying* force initiated* by Webster. The strong influence of the Blue-Back speller [2]**cannot be pinned** on any one factor. The book was uniquely* American, and it was the first of its kind. It filled a void in the national consciousness, which provided a sense of unity within the entire population. The book linked the schoolhouse with the community. Moreover, it connected the poorest child with the highest office in the land, the president of the United States. Furthermore*, the book provided longevity for a new and beginning nation as it was the standard for over one hundred years. Though the changes to the actual English language were few, this small American speller commenced* a literary unification of the country's language that still exists today The days are long over that America [3]**could be mocked**◆ for its lack of language and literature. Now, countless students from around the world come to the United States to learn English and obtain degrees from American Universities. America's language [4]**is** still **called** English and not all that different from England's English, yet there [5]**should be** no doubt that Americans have a strong sense of linguistic nationalism.

Answers Explained

1. The past participle verb form **produced** is required in this AV present perfect verb form pattern. *(PRS HAVE + PST PART)*
2. The past participle verb form **pinned** is required in this PV modal simple verb form pattern.*(MDL + BE + PST PART)*
3. The past participle verb form **mocked** is required in this PV modal simple verb form pattern.*(MDL + BE + PST PART)*
4. The present singular irregular verb form **is** is required in this PV present simple verb form pattern. *(PRS BE + PST PART)*
5. The modal verb form **should** is required in this modal simple verb form pattern. *(MDL + BF)*

CHAPTER 7

PATTERN SHIFTING REVIEW

Grammar Review

5 Practice Edits

One always has enough time,
if one will apply it well.
~Johann Wolfgang von Goethe

Tense Pattern Shifting

Another possible problem with verb patterns is mixing the required elements incorrectly to form unintended or erroneous* patterns. For example, combining a half PV pattern and a half AV pattern is prohibited*. While the simple AV patterns reduce the likelihood of such errors, the more complex AV patterns and all the multi-part PV patterns boost* the possibility of creating pattern shifting errors. Therefore, it is important to make sure the appropriate auxiliary verb or verb participle form is combined correctly to create proper verb form patterns.

Consider the following sentence: "The book has taken by Prof. Undertree."

Does this make sense to you? It shouldn't. Even if the "by Prof. Undertree" doesn't stand out as passive voice, a book can't take anything itself as an inanimate object. So this is clearly a verb pattern error. How would you fix it? "The book has been taken by Prof. Undertree" is one obvious* answer, or "the book was taken by Prof. Undertree" would work as well. It is essential that the patterns are complete and correct for the verbs to make sense to the reader.

Take a look at some of the following pattern shifting mistakes in Chart 21.

CHART 21: PATTERN SHIFTING ERRORS

	PATTERN	ERROR	EXPLAINED	REVISED
AV Continuous	BE + PRS PART	is **edited**	PST PART	is **editing**
AV Perfect	HAVE + PST PART	have **editing**	PRS PART	have **edited**
PV Continuous	BE + PRS PART BE + PST PART	is **been** edited	PST PART BE	is **being** edited
AV Perfect	HAVE + PST PART BE + PST PART	has **being** edited	PRS PART BE	has **been** edited

Review below the example errors and corrections for incorrectly mixed verb patterns.

Pattern Shifting Error Examples

error	I **have taking** many tests in my college classes.
explained	The auxiliary verb form **am** with the present participle **taking** is required for this AV present continuous pattern. *(PRS BE + PRS PART)* The past participle **taken** is required for this AV present perfect pattern. *(PRS HAVE + PST PART)*
revised	1. I **am taking** many tests in my college classes. 2. I **have taken** many tests in my college classes.
error	The TOEFL test **is been taken** all over the world*.
explained	The present participle **being** is required in this PV present continuous pattern. *(PRS BE + PRS PART BE + PST PART)* The auxiliary verb form **have** is required in this PV present perfect pattern. *(PRS HAVE + PST PART BE + PST PART)*
revised	The TOEFL **is being taken** all over the world. The TOEFL **has been taken** all over the world.
error	This test **has being taken** by thousands of students.
explained	The auxiliary verb form **is** is required in this PV present continuous pattern. *(PRS BE + PRS PART BE + PST PART)* The past participle verb form **been** is required in this PV present perfect pattern. *(PRS HAVE + PST PART BE + PST PART)*
revised	This test **is being taken** by thousands of students This test **has been taken** by thousands of students.

Shifting patterns causes confusion and chaos!!

Don't do it!

These examples demonstrate one obvious difficulty with verb form pattern shifting is that there can be multiple correct meanings based on the context of the sentence and paragraph. The most important thing to make sure of is that you don't mix the various patterns and create a verb pattern that does not in fact exist. Which verb tense goes where is a function discussion for another lesson in another book. Here, the point of these exercises is to correctly form the tense patterns to avoid errors. The more quickly you memorize these patterns and match them correctly, the better your writing will be!

Refresh your understanding of this material with the condensed formulas below in Chart 22.

CHART 22: REVIEW MULTI -PART VERB PATTERNS

TENSE		AV	PV
SIMPLE	FORMULA	PST / PRS / FTR	PST / PRS / FTR BE + PST PART
	EXAMPLE	edited / edits / will edit	is edited
CONTINUOUS	FORMULA	PST / PRS / FTR BE + PRS PART	PST / PRS / FTR BE + PRS BE + PST PART
	EXAMPLE	was / am / will be editing	am being edited
PERFECT	FORMULA	PST / PRS / FTR HAVE + PST PART	PST / PRS / FTR HAVE +PST BE + PST PART
	EXAMPLE	have edited	have been edited
PERFECT CONTINUOUS	FORMULA	PST / PRS / FTR HAVE + PST PART BE + PRS PART	
	EXAMPLE	have been editing	

You can see from the Chart 22 that the Passive Voice has a form of "be" in every pattern; there is also always a past participle used. If even one of the pattern's aspects is omitted, errors can occur. For example, if "has taken" is written, this is a fine example of AV present perfect; however, adding the "been" making the verb form pattern "has been taken" changes the voice completely from AV to PV. Realize that every particular verb form pattern has specific requirements that must be followed!

Pattern Shifting Problems Summary

- Each of the verb patterns requires specific parts in a specific order.
- Mixing verb pattern aspects can change voice or meaning.
- Mixing verb pattern aspects creates ambiguity*.
- Mixing the verb pattern aspects creates errors.

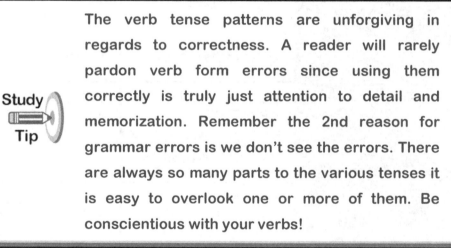

Study Tip

The verb tense patterns are unforgiving in regards to correctness. A reader will rarely pardon verb form errors since using them correctly is truly just attention to detail and memorization. Remember the 2nd reason for grammar errors is we don't see the errors. There are always so many parts to the various tenses it is easy to overlook one or more of them. Be conscientious with your verbs!

Verb Tense Pattern Shifting Practice Edits

These five practice edits will focus on errors with the mixing of verb form patterns or missing required pattern pieces in the verb form. It might be helpful to have your Chart 22: Multi-Part Verb Patterns from page 123 next to you to remind you of the Verb Tense Pattern requirements. Don't forget to check your answers after you complete the edits!

Edit 21: Pattern Shifting
find and fix 4 verb form errors

Raising children in the home was enabled American women to become great interpreters of nonverbal communication (Mehrabian). Because young children cannot speak, their communiqués are expressing through nonverbal indicators. The tone of a cry can mean various things like "I'm hungry" or "I'm lonely." Also, facial expressions can signify everything from "I need a new diaper" to "I don't like peas and carrots." Spending a great deal of time with young children was forced women to pay close attention to these nonverbal signals in order to grasp their children's needs. Even after children learn to speak, they often do not voice all their fears and concerns but express them through body language. Furthermore, teenagers are legendary for communicating in this manner. When teenagers say "I'm fine" standing slouched over with crossed arms and their heads down with eyes to the floor, their body language belies their verbal message. Because women must interpret such body language to effectively communicate with their children, they have becoming masters of nonverbal communication.

Edit 21: Suggested Answers

answers indicated in bold

Raising children in the home [1]**has enabled** American women to become great interpreters of nonverbal communication* (Mehrabian). Because young children cannot speak, their communiqués [2]**are expressed** through nonverbal indicators. The tone of a cry can mean various things like "I'm hungry" or "I'm lonely." Also, facial expressions can signify everything from "I need a new diaper" to "I don't like peas and carrots." Spending a great deal of time with young children [3]**has forced** women to pay close attention to these nonverbal signals in order to grasp their children's needs. Even after children learn to speak, they often do not voice all their fears and concerns but express them through body language. Furthermore, teenagers are legendary for communicating in this manner. When teenagers say "I'm fine" standing slouched over with crossed arms and their heads down with eyes to the floor, their body language belies◆ their verbal message. Because women must interpret such body language to effectively communicate with their children, they [4]**have become** masters of nonverbal communication.

Answers Explained

1. The singular verb form **has** is required in this AV present perfect verb form pattern. *(PRS HAVE + PST PART)*

2. The past participle verb form **expressed** is required in this PV present simple verb form pattern. *(PRS BE + PST PART)*

3. The singular verb form **has** is required in this AV present perfect verb form pattern. *(PRS HAVE + PST PART)*

4. The past participle verb form **become** is required in this AV present perfect verb form pattern. *(PRS HAVE + PST PART)*

Edit 22: Pattern Shifting
find and fix 2 verb form errors

Writing centers, sometimes called writing labs, currently have established in colleges through the United States. These writing centers, with the goals of enabling students to write well independently, fill a significant need in helping college students learn to write (Clark). Most centers provide one-on-one conferencing using the students' own work to assist with the writing process. Because of the methods employed in centers, some people even believe that they are more effective, efficient, and pleasant places to learn to write than the traditional writing classroom (Clark). The current importance of writing centers is even greater today than in previous years as many current students are not simply underprepared but face even greater challenges because English is not their first language. The number of ESL students coming to the writing center has increasing dramatically over the years. Although most college writing centers achieve great success with native English students while employing collaborative methods, these methods are much less successful with ESL students because of their cultural and educational backgrounds, often causing frustration for both students and tutors. A possible solution for this current dilemma is that writing centers change their methods and strategies for tutoring ESL students while colleges also become more involved with and provide more support for ESL learning.

Edit 22: Suggested Answers

answers indicated in Bold

Writing centers, sometimes called writing labs, [1]**are** currently **established** in colleges through the United States. These writing centers, with the goals of enabling students to write well independently, fill a significant* need in helping college students learn to write (Clark). Most centers provide one-on-one conferencing*, using the students' own work to assist with the writing process. Because of the methods employed in centers, some people even believe that they are more effective, efficient, and pleasant places to learn to write than the traditional writing classroom (Clark). The current importance of writing centers is even greater today than in previous years as many current students are not simply underprepared but face even greater challenges* because English is not their first language. The number of ESL students coming to the writing center [2]**has increased** dramatically* over the years. Although most college writing centers achieve great success with native English students while employing collaborative methods, these methods are much less successful with ESL students because of their cultural and educational backgrounds, often causing frustration for both students and tutors. A possible solution for this current dilemma is that writing centers change their methods and strategies for tutoring ESL students while colleges also become more involved with and provide more support for ESL learning.

Answers Explained

1. The present plural irregular verb form **are** is required in this PV present simple verb form pattern. *(PRS BE + PST PART)*

2. The past participle verb form **increased** is required in this AV present perfect verb form pattern. *(PRS HAVE + PST PART)*

Edit 23: Pattern Shifting
find and fix 3 verb form errors

Clearly one of the functions of the Webster's Blue-Back primer was to teach spelling. Because all the children had learning the same spellings of the same words, friendly competitions arose in the classic American scholastic pastime--the spelling bee. Both adults and children enthusiastically were involving in spelling. In the schoolroom, the winner of daily "spell downs" would often earn a small prize such as a coin with a hole drilled in it so that the winner could wear it proudly around her neck. Sometimes the winning child would receive a certificate of accomplishment (Johnston & Withers 172). The truly great spellers could look forward to cross-community spelling competitions. The uniform consistency of the spelling lessons among the schools spread into the community during the friendly spelling competitions that were major social events. The spelling bee was much more than a simple school contest; it was a shared event that involved the entire community. These spelling matches were common events on winter evenings. Webster's Blue-Back Speller was center stage as the authority in any spelling question. The words used in the spelling bee usually were selecting from the Blue-Back Speller. The book not only set a standard for English within the schools, but it also set the same standard in the community at large.

Edit 23: Suggested Answers
answers indicated in bold

Clearly one of the functions of the Webster's Blue-Back primer was to teach spelling. Because all the children [1]**had learned** the same spellings of the same words, friendly competitions arose in the classic American scholastic pastime--the spelling bee. Both adults* and children [2]**were** enthusiastically **involved** in spelling. In the schoolroom, the winner of daily "spell downs" would often earn a small prize such as a coin with a hole drilled in it so that the winner could wear it proudly around her neck. Sometimes the winning child would receive a certificate of accomplishment (Johnston & Withers 172). The truly great spellers could look forward to cross-community* spelling competitions. The uniform* consistency of the spelling lessons among the schools spread into the community during the friendly spelling competitions that were major social events. The spelling bee was much more than a simple school contest; it was a shared event that involved* the entire community. These spelling matches were common events on winter evenings. Webster's Blue-Back Speller was center stage as the authority* in any spelling question. The words used in the spelling bee [3]**were** usually **selected*** from the Blue-Back Speller. The book not only set a standard for English within the schools, but it also set the same standard in the community at large.

Answers Explained

1. The past participle verb form **learned** is required in AV past perfect verb form pattern. *(PST HAVE + PST PART)*
2. The past participle verb form **involved** is required in this PV past simple verb form pattern. *(PST BE + PST PART)*
3. The past participle verb form **selected** is required in this PV past simple verb form pattern. *(PST BE + PST PART)*

Edit 24: Pattern Shifting
find and fix the verb form errors

Similar to John Holt in his essay "How Teachers Make Children Hate Reading," I was read books that were "too hard" for me as a child. One doesn't have to understand all the interpersonal dynamics of feuding families to realize that Romeo and Juliet's parents didn't like each other nor does one have to know all the pitfalls of politics in the modern world to read about Valentine Michael Smith who grew up on Mars and returned to Earth in Robert A. Heinlein's *A Stranger in a Strange Land*. I wish more students would go "exploring for the fun of it" as suggested by Holt. Nonetheless, there are some problems with Holt's ideas. While I completely support the idea of allowing students to read on their own and enjoy the reading, one does have to teach certain ideas and certain structures so that students can be able to advance. Particularly at the college level, specific information must be teaching. I think then what is requiring is both learning the information required in class and learning on one's own. This is why I provide so many resources for students in addition to and supportive of what we do in class. I have also willing to talk to anyone about books at any time and recommend to the best of my ability books that apply to students' interests. For me, my go-to place to get information is a book. Books take me places that I'll never get to go in person. I think like most things loving reading or hating reading is a matter of attitude.

Edit 24: Suggested Answers
answers indicated in bold

Similar to John Holt in his essay "How Teachers Make Children Hate Reading," I [1]**was reading** books that were "too hard" for me as a child. One doesn't have to understand all the interpersonal dynamics of feuding families to realize that Romeo and Juliet's parents didn't like each other nor does one have to know all the pitfalls of politics in the modern world to read about Valentine Michael Smith who grew up on Mars and returned to Earth in Robert A. Heinlein's *A Stranger in a Strange Land*. I wish more students would go "exploring for the fun of it" as suggested by Holt. Nonetheless, there are some problems with Holt's ideas. While I completely support the idea of allowing students to read on their own and enjoy the reading, one does have to teach certain ideas and certain structures so that students can be able to advance. Particularly at the college level, specific information [2]**must be taught**. I think then what [3]**is required** is both learning the information required in class and learning on one's own. This is why I provide so many resources for students in addition to and supportive of what we do in class. I [4]**am** also **willing** to talk to anyone about books at any time and recommend to the best of my ability books that apply to students' interests. For me, my go-to place to get information is a book. Books take me places that I'll never get to go in person. I think like most things loving reading or hating reading is a matter of attitude.

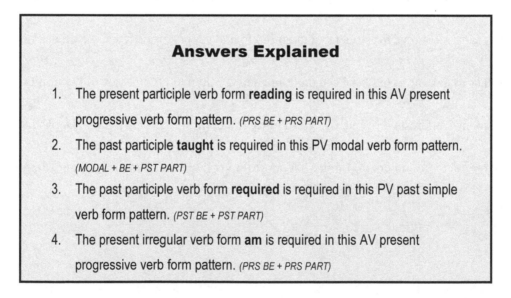

Answers Explained

1. The present participle verb form **reading** is required in this AV present progressive verb form pattern. *(PRS BE + PRS PART)*
2. The past participle **taught** is required in this PV modal verb form pattern. *(MODAL + BE + PST PART)*
3. The past participle verb form **required** is required in this PV past simple verb form pattern. *(PST BE + PST PART)*
4. The present irregular verb form **am** is required in this AV present progressive verb form pattern. *(PRS BE + PRS PART)*

Edit 25: Pattern Shifting
find and fix the verb form errors

Eboo Patel was made a compelling argument for American pluralism in "We Are Each Other's Business." He was based his argument on his experiences with religious diversity and discrimination. He states, "We live in a world where the forces that seek to divide us are strong" (Patel 178). When in high school, Patel, an American Muslim, was confronting with discriminatory anti-Semitic actions against his Jewish friend, he did nothing but sit next to him at the lunch table, offering only a silent presence in his friend's hour of need. This lack of overt support for his friend by doing nothing was been the single most humiliating experience of Patel's life. Now, he knows that pluralism requires the courage to act. Patel claims that belief without action is only an opinion. Because of this lesson, he can prevent such suffering in others; now, he will act. This idea is reminiscent of Edmond Burke's profound idea that evil will win if good men and women do nothing to stop it. Allowing others to hold their beliefs while staying true to one's divergent beliefs, that is a kind of pluralism that I would like to see in my life, my classroom, my state, my country and my world at large. It can certainly be hard to act, to stand up for what is right just because it is right. I guess the key then is simply to realize that my beliefs, if they are truly my beliefs, require actions, not just words, to be real. That is the lesson that I can take from Patel.

Edit 25: Suggested Answers

answers indicated in bold

Eboo Patel [1]**has made** a compelling argument for American pluralism in "We Are Each Other's Business." He [2]**has based** his argument on his experiences with religious diversity and discrimination. He states, "We live in a world where the forces that seek to divide us are strong" (Patel 178). When in high school, Patel, an American Muslim, [3]**was confronted*** with discriminatory anti-Semitic actions against his Jewish friend, Patel, an American Muslim did nothing but sit next to him at the lunch table, offering only a silent presence in his friend's hour of need. This lack of overt support for his friend by doing nothing [4]**has been** the single most humiliating experience of Patel's life. Now, he knows that pluralism requires the courage to act. Patel claims that belief without action is only an opinion. Because of this lesson, he can prevent such suffering in others; now, he will act. This idea is reminiscent of Edmond Burke's profound idea that evil will win if good men and women do nothing to stop it. Allowing others to hold their beliefs while staying true to one's divergent beliefs, that is a kind of pluralism that I would like to see in my life, my classroom, my state, my country and my world at large. It can certainly be hard to act, to stand up for what is right just because it is right. I guess the key then is simply to realize that my beliefs, if they are truly my beliefs, require actions, not just words, to be real. That is the lesson that I can take from Patel.

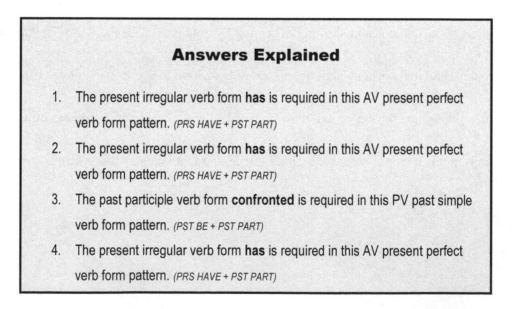

Answers Explained

1. The present irregular verb form **has** is required in this AV present perfect verb form pattern. *(PRS HAVE + PST PART)*
2. The present irregular verb form **has** is required in this AV present perfect verb form pattern. *(PRS HAVE + PST PART)*
3. The past participle verb form **confronted** is required in this PV past simple verb form pattern. *(PST BE + PST PART)*
4. The present irregular verb form **has** is required in this AV present perfect verb form pattern. *(PRS HAVE + PST PART)*

8

COMBINED EDITING PRACTICE

28 Practice Edits

We become what we do.

~Chiang Kai-Shek

Wow, you've worked through the first twenty-five Practice Edits. How did you do? Did you apply the various strategies? Do you have a favorite? Beginning or emerging writers often find Isolation to be the most helpful. Focusing can be great if you already know your weaknesses. The one I use the most is Reading Aloud because it helps me to hear the language and I tend to think out loud as I write. I also try and take breaks as well. Sometimes the sheer effort that good writing requires is overwhelming for all of us! Taking a walk on the beach or binge watching Netflix for a while can help me have perspective on my work. How did you take breaks while editing?

If you've been doing all the previous edits, you've been focusing on only one kind of verb form error at a time; now it gets more real. In authentic writing, we make all kinds of errors at the same time. Hence, it is important to practice looking for and editing all the errors all at the same time. Now, you may be thinking about your own writing and your own errors. More than likely, you have other errors than just verb form. Of course, you do. So do I. Everyone has their own error-making tendencies.

Remember though, we are practicing working on errors in focused isolation in this book. Trying to improve all one's grammar at once can be frustrating and overwhelming. By mastering one kind of error at a time, you can build your success, and before you know it, you'll be the kind of writer you long to be.

Study Tip

The more familiar you are with the patterns (Error Cause 1), the more easily you will see the error in your own writing (Error Cause 2). By practicing extensively editing these patterns, you will be addressing Error Cause 3, and you should see improved results in your editing and writing!

Combined Editing Practice Edits

None of the following edits will indicate the number of errors within. Some edits may even be error free! When I was quickly reviewing the Practice Edits, I missed an error or two. And I wrote them! So be thorough. Don't try and power through this practice. This not a case where speed is your friend!

Think about what happens when you write a graded assignment at the last minute without spending sufficient editing time and receive a less-than-satisfactory grade. That never feels good, does it? You know you could have earned a better grade job with just a little more effort. Similarly, engaging in a slow, deliberate practice now, your improved verb form usage will pay off in the long term.

As you complete the upcoming edits, make sure that you stay focused on the verb forms. If you have a chance to change a noun for subject-verb agreement, you can, but the more correct answer here would be to change the verb. Don't get caught up in looking at prepositions or adverbs or other parts of speech. Those features can be dealt with in another book for another kind of practice. The focus right now is verb form. Keep that in mind as you practice.

Failure is a success
if we learn from it.
~Malcolm Forbes

Edit 26: Combined Verb Forms
find and fix the verb form errors

Too many American families either don't have or don't take the time to explore the important issues that Alice Walker bring out in her novel, The Color Purple. Unfortunately, in today's society, average students spend more time with the media both through TV and movies than in discussion with their families (Knickerbocker). The American media do not hesitate to examine these current issues extensively through its forums of sitcoms, talk shows, and movies. In popular television sitcoms like Friends, both heterosexual and homosexual relationships are explored. On talk shows like Jerry Springer and Sally Jesse Raphael, rape and incest are popular themes. Modern movies also constantly portray people experimenting with religion in such movies as The Craft and Stigmata. Even though the media gives great coverage to these issues, at best its views have biased and, at worst, are completely superficial. Although high school students live in a precarious balance between childhood and adulthood, they are not deaf or blind to the media that permeate modern society and thus cannot avoid being influenced by it. Today's average teenager has more money, time, and freedom than in any other period in American history; this combination of resources adds up to the ability to translate the new ideas offered by the American media into personal experiences with or without adult guidance (Hine).

Edit 26: Suggested Answers

answers indicated in bold

Too many American families either do not have or don't take the time to explore the important issues that Alice Walker [1]**brings** out in her novel, *The Color Purple*. Unfortunately, in today's society, average students spend more time with the media* both through TV and movies than in discussion with their families (Knickerbocker). The American media [2]**does** not hesitate to examine these current issues extensively through its forums of sitcoms, talk shows, and movies. In popular television sitcoms like *Friends,* both heterosexual* and homosexual relationships are explored. On talk shows like *Jerry Springer* and *Sally Jesse Raphael,* rape and incest are popular themes*. Modern movies also constantly* portray people experimenting with religion in such movies as *The Craft* and *Stigmata*. Even though the media gives great coverage to these issues, at best its views [3]**are biased*** and, at worst, are completely superficial. Although high school students live in a precarious balance between childhood and adulthood, they are not deaf or blind to the media that [4]**permeates** modern society and thus cannot avoid being influenced by it. Today's average teenager has more money, time, and freedom than in any other period in American history; this combination of resources adds up to the ability to translate the new ideas offered by the American media into personal experiences with or without adult guidance (Hine).

Answers Explained

1. This singular noun *Walker* requires the singular verb form **brings**. [CH5]
2. This singular collective noun *media* requires the singular form verb **does**. [CH5]
3. The plural verb form **are** is required in this PV present simple verb form pattern. [CH7] *(PRS BE + PAST PART)*
4. The singular referent collective noun *media* requires the singular verb form **permeates**. [CH5]

Edit 27: Combined Verb Forms
find and fix the verb form errors

Although the heroines of Amanda Quick's novels ordinary in appearance, they are not

mediocre in intelligence and skill and use these qualities to overcome many hardships. Quick's

heroines set an influential standard by using logic rather than emotion to reach the desire end as

does Alice in the novel *Mystique*. Alice searches for knowledge as she studies everything from

logic and rhetoric to insects and geology. Rather than fulfilling the traditional role of the helpless

female, Alice goes after what she wants by follow a clearly defined plan. Unfortunately, an

unscrupulous relative steals the inheritance she and her brother had possessed. Although Alice has

no desire to wed but would rather join a convent so she can further her academic studies, she

marries a legendary knight to provide her brother's inheritance. Alice is able to use her powers of

reason to help her husband solve his problems. With her clever wit, she even manages to rescue

her husband from difficult situations: a reversal of the idea that the knight should always come to

the rescue. By the end of the story, everyone is happy, and life is good. This story would not be a

success without Alice's ability to respond to difficult situations calmly and reasonably. Again,

Quick dismisses the helpless female stereotype and empower her heroines to directly affect their

individual fates; while the stories themselves are purely fictional, Alice is an example of how an

empower woman can be both clever and in love.

Edit 27: Suggested Answers

answers indicated in bold

Although the *heroines* of Amanda Quick's novels [1]**are** ordinary in appearance, they are not mediocre in intelligence and skill and use these qualities to overcome many hardships. Quick's heroines set an influential standard by using logic rather than emotion to reach the [2]**desired** end as does Alice in the novel *Mystique*. Alice searches for knowledge as she studies everything from logic and rhetoric to insects and geology. Rather than fulfilling the traditional role of the helpless female, Alice goes after what she wants by [3]**following** a clearly defined* plan. Unfortunately, an unscrupulous relative steals the inheritance she and her brother had possessed. Although Alice has no desire to wed but would rather join a convent so she can further her academic studies, she marries a legendary knight to provide her brother's inheritance. Alice is able to use her powers of reason to help her husband solve his problems. With her clever wit, she even manages to rescue her husband from difficult situations: a reversal of the idea that the knight should always come to the rescue. By the end of the story, everyone is happy, and life is good. This story would not be a success without Alice's ability to respond* to difficult situations calmly and reasonably. Again, Quick dismisses the helpless female stereotype and [4]**empowers** her heroines to directly affect their individual fates; while the stories themselves are purely fictional, Alice is an example of how an [5]**empowered** woman can be both clever and in love.

Answers Explained

1. The plural verb form **are** is required in this AV present simple verb form pattern. [Ch6]
2. The adjective form requires the past participle **desired**. [Ch4]
3. The gerund form requires the present participle verb form **following**. [Ch4]
4. The singular noun Quick requires the singular verb form **empowers**. [CH5]
5. This adjective form requires the past participle verb form **empowered**. [CH4]

Edit 28: Combined Verb Forms
find and fix the verb form errors

In contrast to the self-made man, Arthur Miller's Willy Loman is the everyman, the "low-man" who try to actualize his self-reliance from his lowly station. To Willy, his way is clear; he follows the path of Dave Singleman, an outstanding salesman. In Willy's mind, Singleman's life is the one to be admired, emulated, and even idealize as heroic (Miller). Singleman's success is not measuring by interacting with and surviving in the natural world, nor does he simply make money. Singleman's great achievement is neither physical nor financial; instead, it is social. Singleman can sit in his room, wearing his comfortable green velvet slippers, pick up a phone and by simply talking to people, make a living (Miller). Singleman's ability to earn his keep by talk to others seems to Willy to be the embodiment of self-reliance and of success. Furthermore, the most reveal evidence of Willy's skewed sense of success is his focus on death. With all his muse about Singleman's lifestyle, Willy is most impressing by the turnout at Singleman's funeral (Miller). That so many people would come out to bury a man surely must prove that man's worth and thus, one should strive to have a big funeral. The bigger the funeral, the more obvious that a man is successful and "knowed."

Edit 28: Suggested Answers

answers indicated in bold

In contrast to the self-made man, Arthur Miller's Willy Loman is the everyman, the "low-man" who [1]**tries** to actualize his self-reliance from his lowly station. To Willy, his way is clear; he follows the path of Dave Singleman, an outstanding salesman. In Willy's mind, Singleman's life is the one to be admired, emulated, and even [2]**idealized** as heroic (Miller). Singleman's success [3]**is** not **measured** by interacting* with and surviving in the natural world, nor does he simply make money. Singleman's great achievement is neither physical nor financial; instead, it is social. Singleman can sit in his room, wearing his comfortable green velvet slippers, pick up a phone and by simply talking to people, make a living (Miller). Singleman's ability to earn his keep by [4]**talking** to others seems to Willy to be the embodiment of self-reliance and of success. Furthermore, the most [5]**revealing** evidence of Willy's skewed sense of success is his focus on death. With all his [6]**musing**✢ about Singleman's lifestyle, Willy [7]**is** most **impressed** by the turnout at Singleman's funeral (Miller). That so many people would come out to bury a man surely must prove that man's worth and thus, one should strive to have a big funeral. The bigger the funeral, the more obvious that a man is successful and "[8]**known.**"

Answers Explained

1. The referent pronoun *everyman* requires the singular verb form **tries**. [CH5]
2. The adjective form requires the past participle verb form **idealized**. [CH4]
3. The past participle verb form **measured** is required in this PV present simple pattern. [CH7] *(PRS BE + PST PART)*
4. The gerund form requires the present participle verb form **talking**. [CH4]
5. The adjective form requires the present participle verb form **revealing**. [CH4]
6. The gerund form requires the present participle verb form **musing**. [CH4]
7. The past participle verb form **impressed** is required in this PV present simple pattern. [CH7] *(PRS BE + PST PART)*
8. The past participle verb form **known** is required by this irregular verb. [CH3]

Edit 29: Combined Verb Forms
find and fix the verb form errors

In 1820, the English author Sydney Smith asked, "Who reads an American book?" and then answered with the amusing reply, "No one" (Warfel 52). Though the American Revolution gave the United States independence as a country, Great Britain still held enormous influence over the new nation. The literary ties to England were so deep-seated that Americans were slow to begin writing and publishing their own literature. The country's language, English, seemed to be the property of England. Moreover, a great many of the people were illiterate. While some public education was available, all the books used to teach children were British. To become truly free, America needed a linguistic revolution as well. During this period an American Patriot, Noah Webster, emerged. An educated man and schoolteacher, he realized the new nation needed a cohesive educational plan to gain its own lingua franca. Linguistic self-reliance was needed to create loyalty in the youth to "their own country, and to inspire them with the pride of national character" (Shoemaker 69). Webster understood and thus promoted the importance of educating the young with tools formulated to meet their specific needs. Furthermore, he understood that a national spirit could bring together a wide variety of people under a common standard, and he worked toward this goal his entire life.

Edit 29: Suggested Answers
answers indicated in bold

In 1820, the English author Sydney Smith asked, "Who reads an American book?" and then answered with the amusing reply, "No one" (Warfel 52). Though the American Revolution gave the United States independence as a country, Great Britain still held enormous* influence over the new nation. The literary ties to England were so deep-seated that Americans were slow to begin writing and publishing their own literature. The country's language, English, seemed to be the property of England. Moreover, a great many of the people were illiterate. While some public education was available, all the books used to teach children were British. To become truly free, America needed a linguistic revolution* as well. During this period an American Patriot, Noah Webster, emerged*. An educated man and schoolteacher, he realized the new nation needed a cohesive educational plan to gain its own lingua franca. Linguistic self-reliance was needed to create loyalty in the youth to "their own country, and to inspire them with the pride of national character" (Shoemaker 69). Webster understood and thus promoted* the importance of educating the young with tools formulated to meet their specific needs. Furthermore, he understood that a national spirit could bring together a wide variety of people under a common standard, and he worked toward this goal his entire life.

Answers Explained

NO verb form errors in this paragraph!

Edit 30: Combined Verb Forms
find and fix the verb form errors

Traditionally, American men have spent less time to deeply develop nonverbal communication

skills for the home than women have. The American man has usually worked outside the home, so he

had not has a woman's opportunity to develop the same proficiency in nonverbal communication

(Mehrabian). Generally, a working father only has a few hours a day to spend at home with his

children. This restriction on time is a hindrance to nonverbal communication because a man mays not

have as much opportunity to study and learn his child's various nonverbal signals. For example, a

new father while holding his infant daughter might see a facial expression resembling a smile. He

could then get excited and exclaim to his wife, "Look! She smiled at me." Often the truth is that the

grimace is not a smile, but rather an expression that necessitate the changing of her diaper. Because

the man is not as familiar with these types of expressions as the woman, he often misinterprets them,

which cans cause frustration. Unfortunately, this frustration often grows worse as children learn to

speak, and their nonverbal communication disagrees with their verbal. Misunderstanding such

nonverbal signals can causes a man to quit trying to interpret them and rely on a woman to recognize

and communicate to him any important nonverbal clues.

Edit 30: Suggested Answers
answers indicated in bold

Traditionally, American men have spent less time to deeply develop nonverbal communication skills for the home than women have. The American male has usually worked outside the home, so he [1]**has not had** a woman's opportunity to develop the same proficiency in nonverbal communication (Mehrabian). Generally, a working father only has a few hours a day to spend at home with his children. This restriction* on time is a hindrance to nonverbal communication because a man [2]**may not have** as much opportunity to study and learn his child's various nonverbal signals. For example, a new father while holding his infant daughter might see a facial expression resembling a smile. He could then get excited and exclaim to his wife, "Look! She smiled at me." Often the truth is that the grimace is not a smile, but rather an expression that necessitates the changing of her diaper. Because the man is not as familiar with these types of expressions as the woman, he often misinterprets them, which [3]**can cause** frustration. Unfortunately, this frustration often grows worse as children learn to speak, and their nonverbal communication disagrees with their verbal. Misunderstanding such nonverbal signals [4]**can cause** a man to quit trying to interpret* them and rely on a woman to recognize and communicate to him any important nonverbal clues.

Answers Explained

1. The singular irregular verb form **has** is required in this AV perfect negative verb form pattern. [CH6] *(HAVE + not+ PAST PART)*
2. The modal verb form **may** is required in this modal simple negative verb form pattern. [CH6] *(MDL + not + BF)*
3. The modal verb form **can** is required in this modal simple verb form pattern. [CH6] *(MDL + BF)*
4. The base form **cause** is required in this AV modal simple verb form pattern. [CH6] *(MDL + BF)*

Edit 31: Combined Verb Forms
find and fix the verb form errors

Joseph Conrad's novella, *Heart of Darkness*, is a story full of metaphor with many levels of interpretation. Conrad tells a dark, mysterious story full of symbolism and metaphor because the human "mind cannot grasps [...] the pure emotion and must be prepared" (Wright 144). Thus, Conrad leads readers with caution to the depths of shadows finded in death. Through the use of the story's three characters, the accountant, the manager, and Kurtz, Conrad uses the metaphor of the heart of darkness to examine man's reaction to death as the ultimate darkness. As the readers move down the river into the heart of Africa, each incident first with the accountant, then with the manager, and finally with Kurtz "is one step further of the imagination into the realm of uncharted darkness" (Wright 147). The unchart darkness of the novella is death. Though death comes to all people, how individuals handle the die and dead reveals their hearts to be full of light or full of darkness. Each have gradations of darkness beginning with the accountant's indifference to death and ending with Kurtz's active participation in death. The heart of darkness is "the horror" of man's response and participation in death.

Edit 31: Suggested Answers
answers indicated in bold

Joseph Conrad's novella, *Heart of Darkness*, is a story full of metaphor with many levels of interpretation. Conrad tells a dark, mysterious story full of symbolism and metaphor because the human "mind [1]**cannot grasp** [...] the pure emotion and must be prepared" (Wright 144). Thus, Conrad leads readers with caution to the depths of shadows [2]**found** in death. Through the use of the story's three characters, the accountant, the manager, and Kurtz, Conrad uses the metaphor of the heart of darkness to examine man's reaction[*] to death as the ultimate darkness. As the readers move down the river into the heart of Africa, each incident first with the accountant, then with the manager, and finally with Kurtz "is one step further of the imagination into the realm of uncharted darkness" (Wright 147). The [3]**uncharted** darkness of the novella is death. Though death comes to all people, how individuals handle the [4]**dying** and dead reveals their hearts to be full of light or full of darkness. Each [5]**has** gradations of darkness beginning with the accountant's indifference to death and ending with Kurtz's active participation in death. The heart of darkness is "the horror" of man's response and participation in death.

Answers Explained

1. The base verb form **grasp** is required in this AV modal simple verb form pattern. [CH6] *(MDL + BF)*
2. The past verb form **found** is required by this irregular verb. [CH3]
3. The adjective verb form requires the past participle verb form **uncharted**. [CH4]
4. The gerund form requires the present participle verb form **dying**. [CH4]
5. The singular indefinite pronoun *each* requires the singular verb form **has**. [CH5]

Edit 32: Combined Verb Forms
find and fix the verb form errors

The characters Daisy, in Henry James' *Daisy Miller: A Study* and Huck, in Mark Twain's *Adventures of Huckleberry Finn*, are restless in their desires. Daisy chafes against the order and routine of her middle-class existence and long for adventure. At the comfortable resort where she meets Winterbourne, Daisy yearns for the excitement of society dinners. Although Winterbourne be a stranger, Daisy breaks the conventional behavioral rules and journeys un-chaperoned with him to a castle. When adventures do not present themselves, Daisy attempts to create them. A simple walk through the garden with Winterbourne is not thrill enough, so Daisy asks him to boat with her on the lake at the unseemly hour of 11 o'clock at night. "That's all I want," she explains. "A little fuss" (James 483). Similarly, Huck also crave excitement. He cannot "sit still" even when he's moving. Rafting on the river with a runaway slave, though adventure enough for Jim and probably anyone else, leave Huck wanting more. When they sight the wreck riverboat *Walter Scott*, Huck just has to go aboard and "slink around" (Twain 259). Huck says, "I can't rest, Jim, till we give her [the wreck] a rummaging" (Twain 260). Huck is forever trying "to get a stirring up, some way" (Twain 252). Both characters demonstrates a restless need for excitement throughout their actions in the stories.

Edit 32: Suggested Answers
answers indicated in bold

The characters Daisy, in Henry James' *Daisy Miller: A Study* and Huck, in Mark Twain's *Adventures of Huckleberry Finn*, are restless in their desires. Daisy chafes against the order and routine of her middle-class existence and [1]**longs** for adventure. At the comfortable resort where she meets Winterbourne, Daisy yearns❖ for the excitement of society dinners. Although Winterbourne [2]**is** a stranger, Daisy breaks the conventional behavioral rules and journeys un-chaperoned with him to a castle. When adventures don't present themselves, Daisy attempts to create them. A simple walk through the garden with Winterbourne [3]**is** not **thrilling** enough, so Daisy asks him to boat with her on the lake at the unseemly hour of 11 o'clock at night. "That's all I want," she explains. "A little fuss" (James 483). Similarly, Huck also [4]**craves** excitement. He cannot "sit still" even when he's moving. Rafting on the river with a runaway slave, though adventure enough for Jim and probably anyone else, [5]**leaves** Huck wanting more. When they sight the [6]**wrecked** riverboat *Walter Scott*, Huck just has to go aboard and "slink around" (Twain 259). Huck says, "I can't rest, Jim, till we give her [the wreck] a rummaging" (Twain 260). Huck is forever trying "to get a stirring up, some way" (Twain 252). Both characters [7]**demonstrate** a restless need for excitement throughout their actions in the stories.

Answers Explained

1. This singular noun *Daisy* requires the singular verb form **longs**. [CH5]

2. This singular noun *Winterborn* requires the singular verb form **is**. [CH5]

3. The present participle verb form **thrilling** is required in this AV present continuous verb form pattern. [CH6] *(PRS BE + PRS PART)*

4. This singular noun *Huck* requires the singular verb form **craves**. [CH5]

5. The singular gerund *Rafting* requires the singular verb form **leaves**. [CH5]

6. This adjective form requires the past participle verb form **wrecked**. [CH4]

7. This plural noun *characters* requires the plural verb form **demonstrate**. [CH5]

Edit 33: Combined Verb Forms
find and fix the verb form errors

The heroine's obedient and kind nature in the tale *Beauty and the Beast* enables her to live happily ever after. In Madame de Beaumont's classic fairy tale, a horrible Beast in a lonely castle require the father of a young girl name Beauty to die for the theft of a white rose. Beauty is obedient to the biblical idea of honor your parents and refuse to let her father die, so she volunteers to give herself to the Beast. Even though the presence of the Beast terrifying to young Beauty, she still follows his dictates and respects his authority by allowing him to dine with her. Finally, Beauty's kind nature overcomes her fear of the Beast's appearance, and she agrees to marry him. Because she is compassionate and accept of him, the Beast turns into a handsome prince, and he and Beauty live "together in happiness for a very long time" (De Beaumont 23-26). By fulfilling a woman's stereotypical obedient and kind role, Beauty overcomes obstacles and finds success and happiness.

Edit 33: Suggested Answers
answers indicated in bold

The heroine's obedient and kind nature in the tale *Beauty and the Beast* enables her to live happily ever after. In Madame de Beaumont's classic* fairy tale, a horrible Beast in a lonely castle [1]**requires** the father of a young girl [2]**named** Beauty to die for the theft of a white rose. Beauty is obedient to the biblical idea of [3]**honoring** your parents and [4]**refuses** to let her father die, so she volunteers to give herself to the Beast. Even though the presence of the Beast [5]**is terrifying** to young Beauty, she still follows his dictates and respects his authority by allowing him to dine with her. Finally, Beauty's kind nature overcomes her fear of the Beast's appearance, and she agrees to marry him. Because she [6]**is** compassionate and **accepting** of him, the Beast turns into a handsome prince, and he and Beauty live "together in happiness for a very long time" (De Beaumont 23-26). By fulfilling a woman's stereotypical obedient and kind role, Beauty overcomes obstacles and finds success and happiness.

Answers Explained

1. The singular noun *Beast* requires the singular verb form **requires**. [CH5]
2. The adjective form requires the past participle verb form **named**. [CH4]
3. The gerund form requires the present participle verb form **honoring**. [CH4]
4. The singular noun *Beauty* requires the singular verb form **refuses**. [CH5]
5. The singular irregular verb form **is** is required in this AV present continuous verb form pattern. [CH6] *(PRS BE + PRS PART)*
6. The present participle verb form **accepting** is required in this AV present continuous verb form pattern. [CH6] *(PRS BE + PRS PART)*

Edit 34: Combined Verb Forms
find and fix the verb form errors

Other female stereotypical roles that lead to a happy ending are seed in Charles Perrault's fairy tale *Bluebeard*. In this classic story, the unname heroine is both a helpless and innocent victim of a horrible man's unwholesome desires. From the beginning of the story, the heroine demonstrates her helplessness. Bluebeard demands her or her sister's hand in marriage, and she is helpless to refuse his desire. The woman further demonstrates her helplessness as even in Bluebeard's home she continues to be surrounded by family and friends, yet is seemingly unable to stand alone at all. Her innocence revealed when her curiosity causes her to betray Bluebeard's order not to go into the lock room. Curiosity is such an essential part of the heroine's nature that Perrault undoubtedly uses it in his moral of the story. Even as the heroine betrays Bluebeard, she is helpless and fearful as she "tremblingly open[s] the door" to her destruction (Perrault 44).

Edit 34: Suggested Answers

answers indicated in bold

Other female stereotypical roles that lead to a happy ending ¹**are seen** in Charles Perrault's fairy tale *Bluebeard*. In this classic story, the ²**unnamed** heroine is both a helpless and innocent victim of a horrible man's unwholesome desires. From the beginning of the story, the heroine demonstrates her helplessness. Bluebeard demands her or her sister's hand in marriage, and she is helpless to refuse his desire. The woman further demonstrates* her helplessness as even in Bluebeard's home she continues to be surrounded by family and friends, yet is seemingly unable to stand alone at all. Her innocence ³**is revealed** when her curiosity causes her to betray Bluebeard's order not to go into the ⁴**locked** room. Curiosity is such an essential part of the heroine's nature that Perrault undoubtedly uses it in his moral of the story. Even as the heroine betrays Bluebeard, she is helpless and fearful as she "tremblingly open[s] the door" to her destruction (Perrault 44).

Answers Explained

1. The past participle verb form **seen** is required by this irregular verb. [CH3]

2. This adjective form requires the past participle verb form **unnamed**. [CH4]

3. The present irregular verb form **is** is required in this this PV present simple verb form pattern. [CH6] *(PRS BE + PST PART)*

4. This adjective requires the past participle verb form **locked**. [CH4]

Edit 35: Combined Verb Forms
find and fix the verb form errors

One of the most intriguing short stories are "The Lottery" by Shirley Jackson despite the fact that many students do not like this horrific story because it reveals a darkness in the human spirit that few wants to face. There is no happy ending here. On the morning of June 27th, in a small village of 300 hundred people somewhere in the world, an annual event takes place. It starts at 10 a.m. so that the villagers can be home for lunch. Everyone is required to attend and participate. This year, like every other for as long as they can remember, everyone in the village, even the youngest toddler, stones to death the unlucky winner of the lottery. Why does each kill his wife, mother, friend and neighbor? Basically, they do so for tradition. Though several has suggested giving it up and no one remembers the ritual that once accompanied the event, they continue to participate in it as a civic activity.

Followings tradition without meaning happens not only in fiction but in real life today. People do things that they have always do because they have always done so with little analysis of why it might have been that way. Like in the story, when bad things do not happen to them, they beam and laugh at their good fortune even while killing. This story drives me to understand why things are the way they are, to question authority and rules, and to make my decision for my actions rather than being led by an uninform or uninterested crowd. This story should be read by every educate person who thinks.

Edit 35: Suggested Answers
answers indicated in bold

One of the most intriguing short stories [1]**is** "The Lottery" by Shirley Jackson despite* the fact that many students do not like this horrific story because it reveals a darkness in the human spirit that few [2]**want** to face. There is no happy ending here. On the morning of June 27th, in a small village of 300 hundred people somewhere in the world, an annual* event takes place. It starts at 10 a.m. so that the villagers can be home for lunch. Everyone is required to attend and participate*. This year, like every other for as long as they can remember, everyone in the village, even the youngest toddler, stones to death the unlucky winner of the lottery. Why does each kill his wife, mother, friend and neighbor? Basically, they do so for tradition. Though several [3]**have** suggested giving it up and no one remembers the ritual that once accompanied the event, they continue to participate in it as a civic activity. [4]**Following** tradition without meaning happens not only in fiction but in real life today. People do things that they [5]**have** always **done** because they have always done so with little analysis* of why it might have been that way. Like in the story, when bad things do not happen to them, they beam and laugh at their good fortune even while killing. This story drives me to understand why things are the way they are, to question authority and rules, and to make my decision for my actions rather than being led by an [6]**uninformed** or uninterested crowd. This story should be read by every [7]**educated** person who thinks.

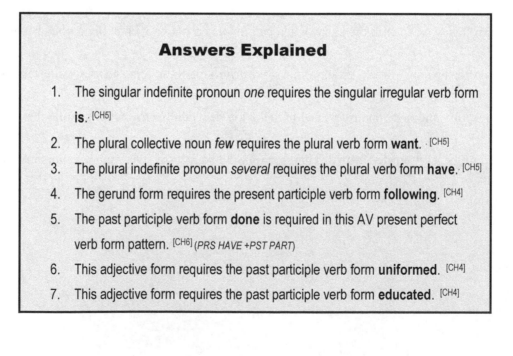

Answers Explained

1. The singular indefinite pronoun *one* requires the singular irregular verb form **is**. [CH5]
2. The plural collective noun *few* requires the plural verb form **want**. [CH5]
3. The plural indefinite pronoun *several* requires the plural verb form **have**. [CH5]
4. The gerund form requires the present participle verb form **following**. [CH4]
5. The past participle verb form **done** is required in this AV present perfect verb form pattern. [CH6] *(PRS HAVE +PST PART)*
6. This adjective form requires the past participle verb form **uniformed**. [CH4]
7. This adjective form requires the past participle verb form **educated**. [CH4]

Edit 36: Combined Verb Forms
find and fix the verb form errors

Ray Bradbury offers a fantastic futuristic story in "Marionettes, Inc." where robots called

marionettes is a reality and affect life in ways unimaginable. Two gentlemen Mr. Braling and Mr.

Smith both finds themselves in unhappy marriages in this story. Mr. Braling blames his wife for his

inability to fulfill his dream of vacationing in Rio, so he employs a marionette, Braling 2, to take his

place and keep his wife happy while he travels the world. Unfortunately for Mr. Braling, Braling 2 is

a sentient being who fall in love with Mrs. Braling. In an unexpect turn of events, Mr. Braling is

thwarted, and Mrs. Braling and Braling 2 live happily ever after. Similarly, Mr. Smith plans to get a

marionette so that he can escape from his smothering wife, just to find out that she has already replace

herself with a marionette and left him. "Be careful what you wish for" is the moral of the story

because you just might get it. Both men wanted to be done with their wives, and both men received

this result. Unfortunately for both, neither outcome was exactly what each had hoped for.

Edit 36: Suggested Answers

answers indicated in bold

     Ray Bradbury offers a fantastic futuristic story in "Marionettes, Inc." where robots called marionettes [1]**are** a reality and affect life in unimaginable ways. Two gentlemen Mr. Braling and Mr. Smith both [2]**find** themselves in unhappy marriages in this story. Mr. Braling blames his wife for his inability to fulfill his dream of vacationing in Rio, so he employs a marionette, Braling 2, to take his place and keep his wife happy while he travels the world. Unfortunately for Mr. Braling, Braling 2 is a sentient being who [3]**falls** in love with Mrs. Braling. In an [4]**unexpected** turn of events, Mr. Braling is thwarted, and Mrs. Braling and Braling 2 live happily ever after. Similarly, Mr. Smith plans to get a marionette so that he can escape from his smothering wife, just to find out that she [5]**has** already **replaced** herself with a marionette and left him. "[6]**Being** careful what you wish for" is the moral of the story because you just might get it. Both men wanted to be done with their wives, and both men received this result. Unfortunately for both, neither outcome* was exactly what each had hoped for.

Answers Explained

1. The plural noun *robots* requires the plural irregular verb form **are**. [CH5]
2. The plural indefinite pronoun *both* requires the plural verb form **find**. [CH5]
3. The singular referent noun *being* requires the singular verb form **falls**. [CH5]
4. The adjective form requires the past participle verb form **unexpected**. [CH4]
5. The past participle verb form **replaced** required in this AV present perfect verb form pattern. [CH6] *(PRS HAVE +PST PART)*
6. The gerund form requires the present participle verb form **being**. [CH4]

Edit 37: Combined Verb Forms
find and fix the verb form errors

O. Henry delivers a nontraditional fairy tale in the "The Last Leaf." Joanna, a young artistic Californian, lives with her painter friend Sue in a Greenwich Village artistic colony to pursue their dreams. The villain of the story is a disease, but not just any disease, the terrible, devastate disease of Pneumonia that takes the lives of hundreds if not thousands of people. This dark, disease stranger who is not a "chivalric old gentleman...stalks about the colony, touching one here and there with his icy fingers" (66). Poor Joanna does not have a chance against "the red-fisted short-breathed old duffer" since after their encounter, she has only a ten percent survival chance (66). Like in all fairy tales, someone rides to her rescue, but the unusual hero is the failed drinked artist Old Behrman, who "scoff[s] terribly at softness in anyone" but wants to protect the two artists who live in the apartment above him. When Old Behrman hears that Joanna thinks she die when the last leaf falls from the vine outside her window, he is enraged at her "idiotic imaginings" (68). In a freeze winter rain, Old Behrman quietly climbs outside her window and paints his only masterpiece, a beautiful, frail leaf clinging to the struggling vine. Upon seeing this determine leaf, Joanna decides to live and slowly begins to get better. Unfortunately, Old Berhman's sacrifice requires his life as he gets sick himself. The damsel in distress is saved, but the hero is not.

Edit 37: Suggested Answers
answers indicated in bold

O. Henry delivers a nontraditional fairy tale in the "The Last Leaf." Joanna, a young artistic Californian, lives with her painter friend Sue in a Greenwich Village artistic colony to pursue* their dreams. The villain of the story is a disease, but not just any disease, the terrible, [1]**devastating** disease of Pneumonia that takes the lives of hundreds if not thousands of people. This dark, [2]**diseased** stranger who is not a "chivalric old gentleman …stalks about the colony, touching one here and there with his icy fingers" (66). Poor Joanna does not have a chance against "the red-fisted short-breathed old duffer" since after their encounter, she has only a ten percent* survival chance (66). Like in all fairy tales, someone rides to her rescue, but the unusual hero is the failed [3]**drunken** artist Old Behrman, who "scoff[s] terribly at softness in anyone" but wants to protect the two artists who live in the apartment above him. When Old Behrman hears that Joanna thinks she [4]**will die** when the last leaf falls from the vine outside her window, he is enraged at her "idiotic imaginings" (68). In a [5]**freezing** winter rain, Old Behrman quietly climbs outside her window and paints his only masterpiece, a beautiful, frail leaf clinging to the struggling vine. Upon seeing this [6]**determined** leaf, Joanna decides to live and slowly begins to get better. Unfortunately, Old Berhman's sacrifice requires his life as he gets sick himself. The damsel in distress is saved, but the hero is not.

Answers Explained

1. The adjective form requires the present participle verb form **devastating**. [Ch4]
2. The adjective form requires the past participle verb form **diseased**. [Ch4]
3. The past participle **drunken** is required by this irregular verb. [CH3]
4. The modal base verb form **will** is required in this simple future verb form pattern. [CH6] *(FTR + BF)*
5. The adjective form requires the present participle verb form **freezing**. [Ch4]
6. The adjective form requires the past participle verb form **determined**. [Ch4]

Edit 38: Combined Verb Forms
find and fix the verb form errors

Cynthia Stewart-Copier tells the inspirational story "If the Dream Is Big Enough, the Facts Don't Count," in which a little girl pursued her seemingly impossible dreams of going to college, yet achieved them through hard work, perseverance, and belief. All throughout elementary school, this girl practiced basketball with the goal of getting a college scholarship. With others and alone, she dribblen and shot that basketball over and over. She played on the varsity team, intent on her goal. Even when the coach told her that at 5' 5" she would never get a scholarship, she played on with the power of her dream. She did receive a scholarship to a NCAA Division I team, where as a freshman she had more playing time than any previous woman at the University. Tragically, her inspiration for her dream, her father, becomed sick and died of cancer. On his death bed, he made her promise she would continue to pursue her dream of a degree. Though it taked her six years rather than the average four, she completed her degree. She was drived by her Father's words, which she made her own: "If the dream is big enough, the facts don't count" (22). Despite her learning disability, her insufficient height, and her father's death, she keeped on pursuing her dream. This story offers a motivate example of how hard work and drive can enable a person to overcome the odds against her to find her success in life. She had the support of her family, but she achieved her dream through her outstand effort and passion.

Edit 38: Suggested Answers
answers indicated in bold

Cynthia Stewart-Copier tells the inspirational story "If the Dream Is Big Enough, the Facts Don't Count," in which a little girl pursued her seemingly impossible dreams of going to college, yet achieved them through hard work, perseverance, and belief. All throughout elementary school, this girl practiced basketball with the goal of getting a college scholarship. With others and alone, she [1]**dribbled** and shot that basketball over and over. She played on the varsity team*, intent on her goal. Even when the coach [2]**told** her that at 5' 5" she would never get a scholarship, she played on with the power of her dream. She did receive a scholarship to a NCAA Division I team, where as a freshman she had more playing time than any previous woman at the University. Tragically, her inspiration for her dream, her father, [3]**became** sick and died of cancer. On his death bed, he made her promise she would continue to pursue her dream of a degree. Though it [4]**took** her six years rather than the average four, she completed her degree. She was [5]**driven** by her Father's words, which she made her own: "If the dream is big enough, the facts don't count" (22). Despite her learning disability, her insufficient height, and her father's death, she [6]**kept** on pursuing her dream. This story offers a [7]**motivating** example of how hard work and drive can enable a person to overcome the odds against her to find her success in life. She had the support of her family, but she achieved her dream through her [8]**outstanding** effort and passion.

Answers Explained

1. The past verb form **dribbled** is required by this regular verb. [CH3]

2. The past verb form **told** is required by this irregular verb. [CH3]

3. The past verb form **became** is required by this irregular verb. [CH3]

4. The past verb form **took** is required by this irregular verb. [CH3]

5. The past participle verb form **driven** is required by this regular verb. [CH3]

6. The past verb form **kept** is required by this irregular verb. [CH3]

7. The adjective requires the present participle verb form **motivating**. [CH4]

8. The adjective form requires the present participle verb form **outstanding**. [CH4]

Edit 39: Combined Verb Forms
find and fix the verb form errors

In "Experiment" Jamie Miles redefines college experimentation. When people think of experimenting in college, some often considers an alternative lifestyle choice with drugs. In fact, an idiomatic English phrase is "experimented with drugs." However, Miles turns over that notion with her story of experimentings with a dance class. As an undefine freshman, a "guppy in a sea of students," Miles seeked to find out who she was and who she could be (45). She tried everything and eventually landed in a swing dance class where she met her boyfriend. Miles recommends that all college students experiment with things, not only the immediate possibilities but also those long-term aspects as well; by doing this, students will "find [their] own currents in a sea of swimming fish" (46). Like Miles, I agree that college can be the place to discover new interests, especially for ESL students. When coming to a new country in a new language, everything is unfamiliar. Some things wills not fit and should be rejected, but some novel experiences might turn out to be the most meaningful aspects of a person's college life. How would one know without trying? Finding one's way often require experimentation.

Edit 39: Suggested Answers
answers indicated in bold

In "Experiment" Jamie Miles redefines college experimentation. When people think of experimenting in college, some often [1]**consider** an alternative lifestyle choice with drugs. In fact, an idiomatic English phrase is "experimented with drugs." However, Miles turns over that notion with her story of [2]**experimenting** with a dance class. As an [3]**undefined** freshman, a "guppy in a sea of students," Miles [4]**sought** to find out who she was and who she could be (45). She tried everything and eventually landed in a swing dance class where she met her boyfriend. Miles recommends that all college students experiment with things, not only the immediate possibilities but also those long-term aspects as well; by doing this, students will "find [their] own currents in a sea of swimming fish" (46). Like Miles, I agree that college can be the place to discover new interests, especially for ESL students. When coming to a new country in a new language, everything is unfamiliar. Some things [5]**will** not **fit** and should be rejected, but some novel experiences might turn out to be the most meaningful aspects of a person's college life. How would one know without trying? Finding one's way often [6]**requires** experimentation.

Answers Explained

1. This plural collective noun *some* requires the plural verb form **consider**. [CH5]
2. The gerund form requires the present participle verb form **experimenting**. [CH4]
3. This adjective form requires the past participle verb form **undefined**. [CH4]
4. The past verb form **sought** is required by this irregular verb. [CH3]
5. The modal verb base form **will** is required in this AV modal simple negative verb form pattern. [CH6] *(MDL + not+ VERB)*
6. This gerund *finding* requires the singular verb form **requires**. [CH5]

Edit 40: Combined Verb Forms
find and fix the verb form errors

Mike Bunn suggests, in "How to Read like a Writer," that I should as a writer "carefully consider the choices the author made and the techniques that he or she used, and then decide whether … to make those same choices or use those same techniques" (73). Here Bunn, in fact, address the larger matter of how ESL students can make their writing not only more academic but also more English sounding. By imitating the style and tone and even some vocabulary of academic writers, student writing is improved. Then, Bunn gives further directions to students by arguing, "you'll have to train yourself to do well" (79). In making this comment, he contend that mastering this new way of writing will be challenging and take time. That idea I know, both from my own writing experience and over ten years of teaching, to be true. Perhaps the most important idea that Bunn offers is on page 83 when he argues that there are no right questions to ask in analyzing a text; instead, students' "own reactions to what [they're] reading will help determine the kinds of questions to ask." In other words, Bunn believes that using others' work as templates is not limiting as long as the students analyze the material sufficiently and apply it to the particular task they given. I believe that learning and efficiently utilizing these skills Bunn presents will greatly enhance one's writing ability.

Edit 40: Suggested Answers

answers indicated in bold

Mike Bunn suggests, in "How to Read like a Writer," that I should as a writer "carefully consider the choices the author made and the techniques that he or she used, and then decide whether to make those same choices or use those same techniques" (73). Here Bunn [1]**is**, in fact, **addressing** the larger matter of how ESL students can make their writing not only more academic but also more English sounding. By imitating the style* and tone and even some vocabulary of academic writers, student writing is improved. Then, Bunn gives further directions to students by arguing, "you'll have to train yourself to do well" (79). In making this comment, he [2]**contends** that mastering this new way of writing will be challenging and take time. That idea I know, both from my own writing experience and over ten years of teaching, to be true. Perhaps the most important idea that Bunn offers is on page 83 when he argues that there are no right questions to ask in analyzing a text; instead, students' "own reactions to what [they're] reading will help determine the kinds of questions to ask." In other words, Bunn believes that using others' work as templates is not limiting as long as the students analyze the material sufficiently and apply it to the particular task they [3]**are given**. I believe that learning and efficiently utilizing these skills Bunn presents will greatly enhance* one's writing ability.

Answers Explained

1. The singular irregular verb form **is** is required in this AV present continuous verb form pattern. [CH6] *(PRS BE + PRS PART)*
2. The singular pronoun *he* requires the singular verb form **contends**. [CH5]
3. The plural irregular verb form **are** is required in this this PV present simple verb form pattern. [CH6] *(PRS BE + PST PART)*

Edit 41: Combined Verb Forms
find and fix the verb form errors

In "How to Read like a Writer," Mike Bunn ask, "Would you want to try the technique [of starting one's writing with a quote] in your own writing?" (73). My response would usually be yes. I often have difficulty starting my writing, yet beginning with a quote give me a launching pad on which to begin my ideas. I like to read others' meaningful quotes because they can be inspiring to me in general. Thus, I have several web pages that I go to when I am looking for quotes. Though today I am an accomplished writer, it was not always so. When I started college, I begun in the beginning-level English classes and had to relearn all the grammar I missed in high school. I believe that good writing can be mastered by anyone who is willing to put in the time and effort. Being in control of one's writing is a powerful skill. So much of our digital world is text based whether it is hard copy or digital. Don't kid yourself; writing is work! One of the great things about taking college writing classes is that the instructor forces the student to produce quality writing. Now, I must is my own instructor and force myself. Regardless, I can do it. Yes, I can!

Edit 41: Suggested Answers

answers indicated in bold

In "How to Read like a Writer," Mike Bunn [1]**asks**, "Would you want to try the technique [of starting one's writing with a quote] in your own writing?" (73). My response would usually be yes. I often have difficulty starting my writing, yet beginning with a quote* [2]**gives** me a launching pad on which to begin my ideas. I like to read others' meaningful quotes because they can be inspiring to me in general. Thus, I have several web pages that I go to when I am looking for quotes. Though today I am an accomplished writer, it was not always so. When I started college, I [3]**began** in the beginning-level English classes and had to relearn all the grammar I missed in high school. I believe that good writing can be mastered by anyone who is willing to put in the time and effort. Being in control of one's writing is a powerful skill. So much of our digital world is text based whether it is hard copy or digital. Don't kid yourself; writing is work! One of the great things about taking college writing classes is that the instructor forces the student to produce quality writing. Now, I [4]**must be** my own instructor and force myself. Regardless, I can do it. Yes, I can.

Answers Explained

1. This singular noun *Bunn* requires the singular verb form **asks**. [CH5]
2. The gerund *beginning* requires the singular verb form **gives**. [CH5]
3. The past verb form **began** is required by this irregular verb. [CH3]
4. The base verb form **be** is required in this AV modal simple verb form pattern. [CH6] *(MDL + BF)*

Edit 42: Combined Verb Forms
find and fix the verb form errors

Poems speak to individuals differently because of whom they are and what they have experienced. That is the beauty and difficulty of poetry. One of the influential poems in my life is a short poem by William Ernest Henley that didn't even have a title when it was first published, Eventually, it was title by an editor and is now calling "Invictus," which is Latin for unconquerable. Henley written this poem while struggling himself with Tuberculosis. Henley wrote, "under the bludgeonings of chance, my head is bloody but unbowed." Like him, I've experienced much grief in my life, most of it due to chance. One example is that my beloved mother had the devastating disease of Multiple Sclerosis (MS) and suffered greatly before passed away in 2014. MS is greatly similar to Henley's "place of wrath and tears," which I suffered watching my mother struggle. While I am glad she is no longer in pain, I miss her every day. Even so, like in the poem, I believe that "I am the master of my fate: I am the captain of my soul." I do not have to allow adversity and sorrow bring me down, but I can rosed and be unafraid. I find poems like this give me strength in times of excruciate pain and grief.

Edit 42: Suggested Answers

answers indicated in bold

Poems speak to individuals differently because of whom they are and what they have experienced. That is the beauty and difficulty of poetry. One of the influential poems in my life is a short poem by William Ernest Henley that didn't even have a title when it was first published, Eventually, it [1]**was titled** by an editor and [2]**is** now **called** "Invictus," which is Latin for unconquerable. Henley [3]**wrote** this poem while struggling himself with Tuberculosis. Henley wrote, "under the bludgeonings of chance, my head is bloody but unbowed." Like him, I've experienced much grief in my life, most of it due to chance. One example is that my beloved mother had the devastating disease of Multiple Sclerosis (MS) and suffered greatly before [4]**passing** away in 2014. MS is greatly similar to Henley's "place of wrath and tears," which I suffered watching my mother struggle. While I am glad she is no longer in pain, I miss her every day. Even so, like in the poem, I believe that "I am the master of my fate: I am the captain of my soul." I do not have to allow adversity and sorrow bring me down, but I **can** [5]**rise** and be unafraid. I find poems like this give me strength in times of [6]**excruciating** pain and grief.

Answers Explained

1. The past participle verb form **titled** is required in this PV past simple verb form pattern. [CH6] *(PST BE + PST PART)*
2. The past participle verb form **called** is required in this PV past simple verb form pattern. [CH7] *(PST BE + PST PART)*
3. The past verb form **wrote** is required by this irregular verb. [CH3]
4. This adjective form requires the present participle verb form **passing**. [CH4]
5. The base verb form **rise** is required in this AV modal simple verb form pattern. [CH6] *(MDL + BF)*
6. This adjective form requires the present participle verb form **excruciating**. [CH4]

Please Note: the noun gerund "bludgeonings" is an exception to the always singular gerund rule just like "feelings." While these plural gerunds are few and far between, they do exist.

Edit 43: Combined Verb Forms
find and fix the verb form errors

I would like to address Shelley Reid's number one principle, in "Ten Ways to Think about Writing: Metaphoric Musings for College Writing Students," where she states that students should, "write about what [they] know about, [and feeling] curious about" (4). Then she goes on to state that writers should write about what they can "find a way to be curious about or interested in" (4). Reid's point here is that it is, in fact, the students' responsibility to make interesting whatever topic given by a classroom instructor. Reid not suggesting that students can write about any topic that they choose; unfortunately, that's not practical in a classroom with twenty-five or more students. What she does advise, though, is within the bounds of the write assignment, it can be possible to find meaning and applicability, and by doing so, the writing will be better. The higher the level students achieve, the more demonstrate freedom they wills have in topic choice. That's the reality of American college.

Edit 43: Suggested Answers

answers indicated in bold

      I would like to address Shelley Reid's number one principle, in "Ten Ways to Think about Writing: Metaphoric Musings for College Writing Students," where she states that students should, "write about what [they] know about, [and [1]**are feeling**] curious about" (4). Then she goes on to state that writers should write about what they can "find a way to be curious about or interested in" (4). Reid's point here is that it is, in fact, the students' responsibility to make interesting whatever topic [2]**is given** by a classroom instructor. Reid [3]**is** not **suggesting** that students can write about any topic that they choose; unfortunately, that's not practical in a classroom with twenty-five or more students. What she does advise, though, is within the bounds of the [4]**writing** assignment, it can be possible to find meaning and applicability, and by doing so, the writing will be better. The higher the level students achieve, the more [5]**demonstrated*** freedom they [6]**will have** in topic choice. That's the reality of American college.

Answers Explained

1. The plural irregular verb form **are** is required in this AV continuous verb form pattern. [CH6] *(PRS BE + PRS PART)*

2. The singular irregular verb form **is** is required in this PV simple verb form pattern. [CH6] *(PRS BE + PST PART)*

3. The singular irregular verb form **is** is required in this AV continuous verb form pattern. [CH6] *(PRS BE + PRS PART)*

4. The adjective form requires the present participle verb form **writing**. [CH4]

5. The adjective form requires the past participle verb form **demonstrated**. [CH4]

6. The modal verb form **will** is required in this modal simple pattern. [CH6] (MDL + BF)

Edit 44: Combined Verb Forms
find and fix the verb form errors

In "Ten Things Every College Professor Hates," Lisa Wade explains specific student behaviors that drive instructors mad and give alternative actions to guarantee their success. I seen all ten of her mentioned behaviors in my own classroom, but I think number two and number ten bother me the most. Number two is "don't ask the professor if you missed anything important during an absence." In my classes, we always have a class calendar with all the daily activities, links, and homework. Updating that calendar is a time consuming and slightly tedious task, yet I consistently do it. Why? It helps keep both the students and me on the same page of where we are in the class and where we going. The only time we don't do something relevant and important to the overall goals of the class is if I have to call out sick and cancel; even then, sometimes there's homework. Thus, when a student asks me Wade's number two question, it drives me a bit crazy. The website is there, every day, so why ask me? I just do not understand that question. Another irritation for me is Wade's number ten: "Don't be too cool for school." As Wade mentions, "Professors and teaching assistants are the top 3% of students. For better or worse, they value education" (Wade). I don't expect my students to understand the lifelong importance of all of the skills I trying to help them develop, but I certainly would like to think they care! I agree with Wade's suggestion that students shoulds show their instructors they care or at least "pretend as if [they] do."

Edit 44: Suggested Answers
answers indicated in bold

In "Ten Things Every College Professor Hates," Lisa Wade explains specific student behaviors that drive instructors mad and [1]**gives** alternative actions to guarantee their success. I [2]**have seen** all ten of her mentioned behaviors in my own classroom, but I think number two and number ten bother me the most. Number two is "don't ask the professor if you missed anything important during an absence." In my classes, we always have a class calendar with all the daily activities, links, and homework. Updating that calendar is a time consuming and slightly tedious task, yet I consistently do it. Why? It helps keep both the students and me on the same page of where we are in the class and where we [3]**are going**. The only time we don't do something relevant and important to the overall goals of the class is if I have to call out sick and cancel; even then, sometimes there's homework. Thus, when a student asks me Wade's number two question, it drives me a bit crazy. The website* it there, every day, so why ask me? I just do not understand that question. Another irritation for me is Wade's number ten: "Don't be too cool for school." As Wade mentions, "Professors and teaching assistants are the top 3% of students. For better or worse, they value education" (Wade). I don't expect my students to understand the lifelong importance of all of the skills I [4]**am trying** to help them develop, but I certainly would like to think they care! I agree with Wade's suggestion that students [5]**should show** their instructors they care or at least "pretend as if [they] do."

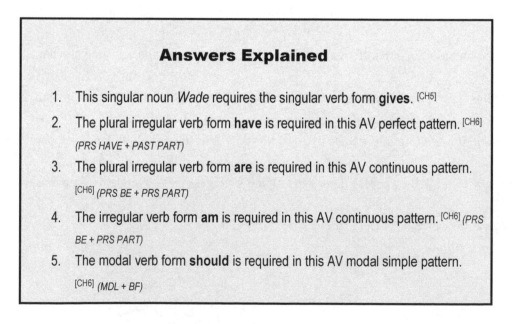

Answers Explained

1. This singular noun *Wade* requires the singular verb form **gives**. [CH5]

2. The plural irregular verb form **have** is required in this AV perfect pattern. [CH6] *(PRS HAVE + PAST PART)*

3. The plural irregular verb form **are** is required in this AV continuous pattern. [CH6] *(PRS BE + PRS PART)*

4. The irregular verb form **am** is required in this AV continuous pattern. [CH6] *(PRS BE + PRS PART)*

5. The modal verb form **should** is required in this AV modal simple pattern. [CH6] *(MDL + BF)*

Edit 45: Combined Verb Forms
find and fix the verb form errors

If I can teach one poem in class, my go-to choice, because it is so universally understandable, is "The Road Not Taken," by Robert Frost. Frost writed, "Two roads diverged in a wood, …I took the one less traveled by, and that has made all the difference." This less traveled road has been a well-discussed feature of this famous work. Nonetheless, what I find fascinatings about this poem is that both of his paths were so similar that it was difficult to distinguish between them. Frost wrote that those "passing there had weared them really about the same." He suggests that it was impossible to tell the difference between the two paths. Frost knowed that he had to choose because there would not be time to walk both paths although he wanted to. Hence, he made a choice. I do not think it is the road itself that made all the difference. Instead, I think it is the act of choosing that made all the difference. Sometimes in life, we simply cannot accomplish all we would hope to, and we have to choose. Personally, I am at a point in my life where I must make a choice; for better or worse, a path must be choosed. The path that I chose will make all the difference, and all I can do is hope that "ages and ages hence" I will happy with the choice I made.

Edit 45: Suggested Answers
answers indicated in bold

If I can teach one poem in class, my go-to choice, because it is so universally understandable, is "The Road Not Taken," by Robert Frost. Frost [1]**wrote**, "Two roads diverged in a wood, …I took the one less traveled by, and that has made all the difference." This less traveled road has been a well-discussed feature* of this famous work. Nonetheless, what I find [2]**fascinating** about this poem is that both of his paths were so similar that it was difficult to distinguish between them. Frost wrote that those "passing there [3]**had worn** them really about the same." He suggests that it was impossible to tell the difference between the two paths. Frost [4]**knew** that he had to choose because there would not be time to walk both paths although he wanted to. Hence, he made a choice. I do not think it is the road itself that made all the difference. Instead, I think it is the act of choosing that made all the difference. Sometimes in life, we simply cannot accomplish all we would hope to, and we have to choose. Personally, I am at a point in my life where I must make a choice; for better or worse, a path [5]**must be chosen**. The path that I chose will make all the difference, and all I can do is hope that "ages and ages hence" I [6]**will be** happy with the choice I made.

Answers Explained

1. The past verb form **wrote** is required by this irregular verb. [CH3]

2. The gerund form requires the present participle verb form **fascinating.** [CH4]

3. The past participle verb form **worn** is required by this irregular verb. [CH3]

4. The past verb form **knew** is required by this irregular verb. [CH3]

5. The past participle verb form **chosen** is required by this irregular verb. [CH3]

6. The base verb form **be** is required in this AV modal simple pattern. [CH6]

    (MDL + BF)

Edit 46: Combined Verb Forms
find and fix the verb form errors

Originally published in 1951, Isaac Asimov's short story "The Fun They Had" paints a picture of the 2155 classroom; although this future doesn't yet exist, there are glimmers that it could soon. In that future, children are taught individually by machines that is "adjusted to fit the mind of each boy and girl" that they teach because "each kid has to be taught differently" (93). In the story, two children name Tommy and Margie discover an astonishing treasure: a paper book about a school where children attended together and were teached by a man. The youth beed astonished by the very idea. Asimov's future is at the opposite end of the current pendulum swing of today's education. There, everyone is an individual while today it seems more and more that everyone is expected to be the same, in learning the same way in the same amount of time, whether or not that is an effective practice. We have come a long way from the ancient Greek model of a few students with one instructor; in today's college, individualize instruction is rare. A current typical college class could have as few as 25 students and as many as 200. Nonetheless, one on one with a computer lacks in many positive aspects of learnings as well. While there is no perfect way to learn, I dream of a world where everyone's needs can be meeted somehow, where everyone has the opportunity to learn, and where everyone has the chance to be successful. If I were writing a story of the classroom of the future, that is the story I would like to write.

Edit 46: Suggested Answers
answers indicated in bold

Originally published in 1951, Isaac Asimov's short story "The Fun They Had" paints a picture of the 2155 classroom; although this future doesn't yet exist, there are glimmers that it could soon. In that future, children are taught individually by machines that [1]**are** "**adjusted***" to fit the mind of each boy and girl" that they teach because "each kid has to be taught differently" (93). In the story, two children [2]**named** Tommy, and Margie discover an astonishing treasure: a paper book about a school where children attended together and [3]**were taught** by a man. The youth [4]**are astonished** by the very idea. Asimov's future is at the opposite end of the current pendulum swing of today's education. There, everyone is an individual while today it seems more and more that everyone is expected to be the same, in learning the same way in the same amount of time, whether or not that is an effective practice. We have come a long way from the ancient Greek model of a few students with one instructor; in today's college, [5]**individualized** instruction is rare. A current college class today could have as few as 25 students and as many as 200. Nonetheless, one on one with a computer lacks in many positive aspects of [6]**learning** as well. While there is no perfect way to learn, I dream of a world where everyone's needs [7]**can be met** somehow, where everyone has the opportunity to learn, and where everyone has the chance to be successful. If I were writing a story of the classroom of the future, that is the story I would like to write.

Answers Explained

1. The plural referent noun *machines* form requires the plural irregular verb form **are**. [CH5]
2. This adjective form requires the past participle verb form **named**. [CH4]
3. The past participle verb form **taught** is required by this irregular verb. [CH3]
4. The past verb form **are** is required by this irregular verb. [CH3]
5. The adjective form requires the past participle verb form **individualized**. [CH4]
6. The gerund form requires the present participle verb form **learning**. [CH4]
7. The past verb form **met** is required by this irregular verb. [CH3]

Please Note: "If I were writing a story" is using the unreal conditional tense; more information on this and other tenses will be available in Editing Academic Texts Advanced Verb Tense.

Edit 47: Combined Verb Forms
find and fix the verb form errors

It is the peaceful, good times that shape us, that we long for, and that we remember, or at least, that is what we tend to think. However, according to Kay Redfield Jamison, in "The Benefits of Restlessness and Jagged Edges," "suffering instruct[s] us in ways less intense emotions can never do" (126). Jamison has bipolar disorder that give her a "frightening, chaotic, and emotional ride" in life (127). She has learned through her experiences that a person cannot escape who she is, so she must accept "the jagged edges and pain" in life (Jamison 127). Jamison claims, "It is best to acknowledge [one's temperament] to accept and to admire the diversity of temperaments Nature has dealt us" (127). I can relate to Jamison's envy of others' calmness. In my entire life, tranquil is not an adjective anyone has ever usen to describe me either. Intense, drived, passionate - these are the adjectives that I've embraced. I've often seed others serenely going about their actions and longed to have that quality in my life. I have even attempt to copy a calm presence, but it never worked out the way I had hoped. Jamison suggests to avoid a boring life, "one ought to be on good terms with one's darker side and one's darker energies" (127-128). Perhaps all I can hope for is to incorporate wisdom to give me what Jamison calls a "cool mind" to go with the discipline I do possess. Fundamentally, we are all what we are, for good and for bad. At least with those jagged edges, life is never bored!

Edit 47: Suggested Answers

answers indicated in bold

It is the peaceful, good times that shape us, that we long for, and that we remember or at least, that is what we tend to think. However, according to Kay Redfield Jamison, in "The Benefits of Restlessness and Jagged Edges," "suffering instruct[s] us in ways less intense* emotions can never do" (126). Jamison has bipolar disorder that **¹gives** her a "frightening, chaotic, and emotional ride" in life (127). She has learned through her experiences that a person cannot escape who she is, so she must accept "the jagged edges and pain" in life (Jamison 127). Jamison claims, "It is best to acknowledge* [one's temperament] to accept and to admire the diversity of temperaments Nature has dealt us" (127). I can relate to Jamison's envy of others' calmness. In my entire life, tranquil is not an adjective anyone **²has** ever **used** to describe me either. Intense, **³driven**, passionate- these are the adjectives that I've embraced. I've⁴ often **seen** others serenely going about their actions and longed to have that quality in my life. I **⁵have** even **attempted** to copy a calm presence, but it never worked out the way I had hoped. Jamison suggests to avoid a boring life, "one ought to be on good terms with one's darker side and one's darker energies" (127-128). Perhaps all I can hope for is to incorporate wisdom to give me what she calls a "cool mind" to go with the discipline I do possess. Fundamentally, we are all what we are, for good and for bad. At least with those jagged edges, life is never **⁶boring**!

Answers Explained

1. The singular referent noun *disorder* requires the singular verb form **gives**. [CH5]

2. The past verb form **used** is required by this regular verb. [CH3]

3. The past participle verb form **driven** is required by this irregular verb. [CH3]

4. The past participle verb form **seen** is required by this irregular verb. [CH3]

5. The past participle verb form **attempted** is required in this AV present perfect pattern. [CH6] *(PRS HAVE +PST PART)*

6. This adjective form requires the present participle verb form **boring**. [CH4]

Edit 48: Combined Verb Forms
find and fix the verb form errors

Dr. Anthony Fauci's article "A Goal of Service to Humankind" explains the three guiding

principles that he has live his life by. His second directing guideline is the principle of excellence.

Fauci declares that he is concerned not only with the big issues in life but the minutiae as well; in fact,

he makes no apology for his attention to detail that causes him a "nagging sense of inadequacy" (66).

Fauci argues that this by-product of being a perfectionist "creates a healthy tension that serves as the

catalyst that drives [him] to fulfill [his] limited potential." (66). Thus, he lives his life as if failure is

not an option. Sometimes in this modern life we confronted by failure. A job interview doesn't

produce the hoped-for career, or a relationship ends badly. Others may suggest the dreams that we

strive for are unobtainable and that we should settle for what we can do, not what we want to do.

Personally, I am often advised to relax or not work as hard in my own life. There is even an entire

popular philosophy, explain in a book by Richard Carlson, of "not sweating the small stuff" or not

worrying about the details that can't be controlled. Fauci, however, does worry. He strives for

excellence in his life-long pursuit of public health. He has took up the fight against the HIV-AIDS

epidemic for the good of the global society. While my goals are not as impactful as his, I hope to be

like him and "accept nothing short of excellence" in my own life pursuits (67).

Edit 48: Suggested Answers

answers indicated in bold

Dr. Anthony Fauci's article "A Goal of Service to Humankind" explains the three guiding principles that he [1]**has lived** his life by. His second directing guideline is the principle of excellence. Fauci declares that he is concerned not only with the big issues in life but the minutiae* as well; in fact, he makes no apology for his attention to detail that causes him a "nagging sense of inadequacy" (66). Fauci argues that this by-product of being a perfectionist "creates a healthy tension that serves as the catalyst that drives [him] to fulfill [his] limited potential." (66). Thus, he lives his life as if failure is not an option*. Sometimes as in this modern life we [2]**are confronted** by failure. A job* interview doesn't produce the hoped-for career, or a relationship ends badly. Others may suggest the dreams that we strive for are unobtainable and that we should settle for what we can do, not what we want to do. Personally, I am often advised to relax or not work as hard in my own life. There is even an entire popular philosophy*, [3]**explained** in a book by Richard Carlson, of "not sweating the small stuff" or not worrying about the details that can't be controlled. Fauci, however, does worry. He strives for excellence in his life-long pursuit of public health. He [4]**has taken** up the fight against the HIV-AIDS epidemic for the good of the global society. While my goals are not as impactful* as his, I hope to be like him and "accept nothing short of excellence" in my own life pursuits (67).

Answers Explained

1. The past participle verb form **lived** is required in this AV perfect pattern. [CH6]
   (PRS HAVE + PST PART)
2. The plural irregular verb form **are** is required in this PV simple pattern. [CH6]
   (PRS BE + PST PART)
3. This adjective form requires the past participle verb form **explained**. [CH4]
4. The past participle verb form **taken** is required in this AV perfect pattern. [CH6]
   (PRS HAVE + PST PART)

Edit 49: Combined Verb Forms
find and fix the verb form errors

Will Kein narrates an amaze tale of learning in his piece "A Not-So-Random Act of Kindness."

As a motivational college speaker, he has encountered millions of students, who performed kind acts

for others like giving blood to those in need, donating money to help other troubled students, and

reaching out to the community. In his story, he tell of the experience when a student helped Kein with

his sick son. He himself is inspired by her unsolicit and unrewarded actions. She helped him just to be

kind, not to get anything in return. Her instructing him was the motivating lesson he learned here.

Kein believes that in education, both student and instructor grows together. Many shares Kein's

belief. While in my class I may be the grammar or writing expert, I am certainly not the expert in

everything. I learn things from my students every class. I think when everyone come together in

kindness with open minds, change can happen. I am grateful to be in the classroom to see those

changes happen! I agree with Dean Robert Schaffer, who stated, "My life has become richer because

of my students" (Kein 189). I too am extremely wealthy in experiences because of my students.

Edit 49: Suggested Answers

answers indicated in bold

Will Kein narrates an [1]**amazing** tale of learning in his piece "A Not-So-Random* Act of Kindness." As a motivational college speaker, he has encountered millions of students, who performed kind acts for others like giving blood to those in need, donating money to help other troubled students, and reaching out to the community. In his story, he [2]**tells** of the experience when a student helped Kein with his sick son. He himself is inspired by her [3]**unsolicited** and unrewarded actions. She helped him just to be kind, not to get anything in return. Her instructing him was the motivating lesson he learned here. Kein believes that in education, both student and instructor [4]**grow** together. Many [5]**share** Kein's belief. While in my class I may be the grammar or writing expert*, I am certainly not the expert in everything. I learn things from my students every class. I think when everyone [6]**comes** together in kindness with open minds, change can happen. I am grateful to be in the classroom to see those changes happen! I agree with Dean Robert Schaffer, who stated, "My life has become richer because of my students" (Kein 189). I too am extremely wealthy in experiences because of my students.

Answers Explained

1. This adjective form requires the present participle verb form **amazing**. [CH4]
2. The singular pronoun *he* requires the singular verb form **tells**. [CH5]
3. This adjective form requires the past participle verb form **unsolicited**. [CH4]
4. The plural indefinite pronoun *both* requires the plural verb form **grow**. [CH5]
5. The plural indefinite pronoun *many* requires the plural verb form **share**. [CH5]
6. The singular indefinite pronoun *everyone* requires the singular verb form **comes**. [CH5]

Edit 50: Combined Verb Forms
find and fix the verb form errors

In the narrative story "Never Say Never," Rosa Torcasino recounts the moment in her life when her dreams becomed reality. Torcasino was always desired to be a teacher and worked tirelessly toward that goal; however, her lack of financial resources seemed insurmountable for achievings her goal of attending the University of Connecticut. Nonetheless, she applied for every scholarship and bit of financial aid she could, despite being just an average student. Not only did she get into the school, but she also was award two scholarships for her tuition. Now with a job and her scholarships, she is a junior at the University and will soon become a teacher. She gives advice to others to "reach for the sky, because if you should happen to miss, you'll still be among the stars" (8). I can truly relate to Torcasino's story myself. I too wanted to become an instructor and struggled with finances. Like her, I worked while in college. Like her, I also got scholarships though I also taked out student loans to fund my education. I believe that diligent hard work can lead to success. If Torcasino can achieve it and if I can achieve it, then others can be successful too!

Edit 50: Suggested Answers
answers indicated in bold

In the narrative story "Never Say Never," Rosa Torcasino recounts the moment in her life when her dreams [1]**became** reality. Torcasino [2]**had** always **desired** to be a teacher and worked tirelessly toward that goal; however, her lack of financial resources seemed insurmountable for [3]**achieving** her goal of attending the University of Connecticut. Nonetheless, she applied for every scholarship and bit of financial aid she could, despite being just an average student. Not only did she get into the school, but she also [4]**was awarded** two scholarships for her tuition. Now with a job and her scholarships, she is a junior at the University and will soon become a teacher. She gives advice to others to "reach for the sky, because if you should happen to miss, you'll still be among the stars" (8). I can truly relate to Torcasino's story myself. I too wanted to become an instructor and struggled with finances*. Like her, I worked while in college. Like her, I also got scholarships though I also [5]**took** out student loans to fund my education. I believe that diligent hard work can lead to success. If Torcasino can achieve it and if I can achieve it, then others can be successful too!

Answers Explained

1. The past verb form **became** is required by this irregular verb. [CH3]
2. The auxiliary verb form have should be **had** is required in this AV present perfect pattern. [CH7] *(PST HAVE +PST PART)*
3. The gerund form requires the present participle **achieving**. [CH4]
4. The past participle verb form **awarded** is required in this PV past simple pattern. [CH6] *(PST BE + PST PART)*
5. The past verb form **took** is required by this irregular verb. [CH3]

Edit 51: Combined Verb Forms
find and fix the verb form errors

By September 2016, doom and gloom media reports had be dominating the presidential primaries

for months. The very future of America seemed to be at stake. In these emotionally charged moments,

Josh Rittenberg's essay "Tomorrow Will Be a Better Day" is a breath of positively charge fresh air.

Rittenberg is a modern teenager, having grown up in a Post 9/11 America, yet he is not weighed

down nor worried about a lack of future. Instead, he is optimistic that he, and we, can learn from past

historical mistakes. He believes that "tomorrow will be a better day- that the world [his] generation

grows into is going to get better, not worse" (Rittenberg 195). While it may be sometimes difficult to

imagine a world without discrimination, hate crimes, and war, it is no more difficult than it would

have been in the 1940s to imagine a man walking on the moon or in the 1980s to imagine the instant

world-wide communication available online today. Rittenberg's argument gives me hope. We are

accomplished great things in response to terrible times. We can continue to do that in the future. I

want to believe in a better world -- a world where people accept differences and allow, even

encourage, those differences, a world where religious preferences are simply personal choices people

make, and a world that are a better place for all. Rittenberg with the optimism of youth believes this is

possible; I want to believe it too.

Edit 51: Suggested Answers
answers indicated in bold

By September 2016, doom and gloom media reports [1]**had been dominating*** the 2016 presidential primaries for months. The very future of America seemed to be at stake. In these emotionally charged moments, Josh Rittenberg's essay "Tomorrow Will Be a Better Day" is a breath of positively [2]**charged** fresh air. Rittenberg is a modern teenager, having grown up in a Post 9/11 America, yet he is not weighed down nor worried about a lack of future. Instead, he is optimistic that he, and we, can learn from past historical mistakes. He believes that "tomorrow will be a better day- that the world [his] generation* grows into is going to get better, not worse" (Rittenberg 195). While it may be sometimes difficult to imagine a world without discrimination, hate crimes, and war, it is no more difficult than it would have been in the 1940s to imagine a man walking on the moon or in the 1980s to imagine the instant world-wide communication available online today. Rittenberg's argument gives me hope. We [3]**have accomplished** great things in response to terrible times. We can continue to do that in the future. I want to believe in a better world -- a world where people accept differences and allow, even encourage, those differences, a world where religious preferences are simply personal choices people make, and a world that [4]**is** a better place for all. Rittenberg with the optimism of youth believes this is possible; I want to believe it too.

Answers Explained

1. The past participle **been** is required in this AV present perfect continuous pattern. [CH6] *(PRS HAVE +PST PART BE +PRS PART)*
2. This adjective form requires the past participle verb form **charged**. [CH4]
3. The auxiliary verb form **have** is required in this AV present perfect pattern. [CH7] *(PRS HAVE +PST PART)*
4. The singular referent noun *world* requires the singular irregular verb form **is**. [CH5]

Edit 52: Combined Verb Forms
find and fix the verb form errors

Fifty years ago, George Mardikian wrote the article "Why I Close My Restaurant" that is still inspiring today. Mardikian explains how he and his family in his restaurant has incorporated his Armenian birth culture with his newly adopted American culture to create a new comprehensive whole. In today's finger pointing, often divisive atmosphere, Mardikian paints a more optimistic picture of what America is. He argues, "Each national group have brought something of its heritage in the form of thousands of different customs, which have become integral parts life in this country" (Mardikian 153). In his America, the cultural variances are a strength rather than a weakness. In his America, "love and mutual respect are fostered and encouraged" (Mardikian 155). That too is my America. It is for that America that I became a writing instructor, specializing in help students master the language and culture needed to succeed in an American college. It is why I embrace all my students' cultures and enjoy learning about the differences. It is the very differences that show me how much the same we all are. Yes, the food, the holidays, the music, or even the language itself may differs. However, the smile of the stranger can be the same for everyone. America has been good to me. Like Mardikian, I want to contribute to the well-being of others. He did so through his restaurant while I do so in my classroom; nonetheless, the result can be the same for us both: a stronger, inclusive place to live.

Edit 52: Suggested Answers
answers indicated in bold

Fifty years ago, George Mardikian wrote the article "Why I Close My Restaurant" that is still inspiring today. Mardikian explains how he and his family in his restaurant [1]**have incorporated** his Armenian birth culture with his newly adopted American culture to create a new comprehensive whole. In today's finger pointing, often divisive atmosphere, Mardikian paints a more optimistic picture of what America is. He argues, "Each national group [2]**has brought** something of its heritage in the form of thousands of different customs, which have become integral parts life in this country" (Mardikian 153). In his America, the cultural variances are a strength rather than a weakness. In his America, "love and mutual* respect are fostered and encouraged" (Mardikian 155). That too is my America. It is for that America that I became a writing instructor, specializing in [3]**helping** students master the language and culture needed to succeed in an American college. It is why I embrace all my students' cultures and enjoy learning about the differences. It is the very differences that show me how much the same we all are. Yes, the food, the holidays, the music, or even the language itself [4]**may differ**. However, the smile of the stranger can be the same for everyone. America has been good to me. Like Mardikian, I want to contribute* to the well-being of others. He did so through his restaurant while I do so in my classroom; nonetheless, the result can be the same for us both: a stronger, inclusive place to live.

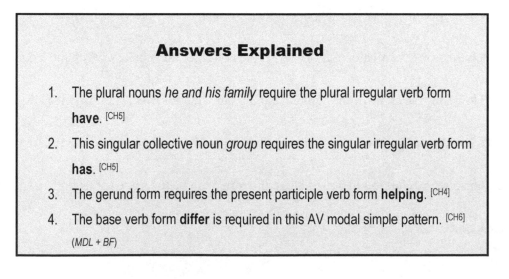

Answers Explained

1. The plural nouns *he and his family* require the plural irregular verb form **have**. [CH5]

2. This singular collective noun *group* requires the singular irregular verb form **has**. [CH5]

3. The gerund form requires the present participle verb form **helping**. [CH4]

4. The base verb form **differ** is required in this AV modal simple pattern. [CH6] (MDL + BF)

Edit 53: Combined Verb Forms
find and fix the verb form errors

Colin Powell have had an illustrious public career, most recently as Secretary of State in 2005, and writes of his beliefs in "The America I Believe In." His America is "a land of immigrants; a nation that has been touched by every nation and … in turn, touch[es] every nation" (Powell 185). Powell's America is the one that I too believe in; this is the America that inspire me to continue teaching despite the difficulties therein. Powel goes on to state that "our greatest strength in dealing with the world is the openness of our society and the welcome nature of our people" (185). In my classroom, I am able to have a similar strength as I encourage students to incorporate their ideas, values, and standards into the American academic way of doing things. I choose to be open to the divergent cultures that come through my doors. However, this is not always the case in our conflict country; not everyone today is welcoming of that very diversity that has maked us Americans who we are today. Powel explains that we, unfortunately, today give the impression that we are "no longer a welcoming nation" (185). Despite what occurred on 9/11, despite what is occurring with ISIS in the world today, despite the mass shooting instances that have be occurring more frequently, Powel claims, "our attitude has to be: We are glad you [tourists, foreigners, and immigrants] are here. We must be careful, but we must not be afraid" (185). We must overcome our fear of other and return to the truth: inclusion, not exclusion, is the American way.

Edit 53: Suggested Answers

answers indicated in bold

Colin Powell **¹has had** an illustrious public career, most recently as Secretary of State in 2005, and writes of his beliefs in "The America I Believe In." His America is "a land of immigrants; a nation that has been touched by every nation and … in turn, touch[es] every nation" (Powell 185). Powell's America is the one that I too believe in; this is the America that **²inspires** me to continue teaching despite the difficulties therein. Powel goes on to state that "our greatest strength in dealing with the world is the openness of our society and the **³welcoming** nature of our people" (185). In my classroom, I am able to have a similar strength as I encourage students to incorporate their ideas, values, and standards into the American academic way of doing things. I choose to be open to the divergent cultures that come through my doors. However, this is not always the case in our **⁴conflicted*** country; not everyone today is welcoming of that very diversity that **⁵has made** us Americans who we are today. Powel explains that we, unfortunately, today give the impression that we are "no longer a welcoming nation" (185). Despite what occurred on 9/11, despite what is occurring with ISIS in the world today, despite the mass shooting instances that **⁶have been occurring** more frequently, Powel claims, "our attitude has to be: We are glad you [tourists, foreigners, and immigrants] are here. We must be careful, but we must not be afraid" (185). We must overcome our fear of other and return to the truth: inclusion, not exclusion, is the American way.

Answers Explained

1. This singular noun *Powel* requires the singular irregular verb form **has**. [CH5]

2. The singular referent noun requires the singular verb form **inspires**. [CH5]

3. This adjective form requires the present participle verb form **welcoming**. [CH5]

4. This adjective form requires the past participle verb form **conflicted**. [CH5]

5. The past participle verb form **made** is required by this irregular verb. [CH3]

6. The past participle verb form **been** is required in this AV present perfect continuous pattern. [CH6] *(PRS HAVE +PST PART BE +PRS PART)*

CHAPTER **9**

FINAL NOTES

So What?

Thanks For Coming!

So Long For Now!

The truth of the matter is
you always know the right thing to do.
The hard part is doing it.
   ~H. Norman Schwarzkopf

So What?

Ernest Hemingway facetiously* once said, "There is nothing to writing. All you do is sit down at a typewriter and bleed." Many ESL students trying to improve their academic writing would agree with Hemingway's assessment that writing hurts so much as to cause bleeding.

Writing well is an arduous* process for everyone, but is a momentous* endeavor for ESL students. Equivalently*, my ESL classroom students struggle with their language. They often despair at ever improving in their usage of grammar. Nonetheless, by the end of an 18-week semester, those students who learn what I teach and practice the exercises I assign absolutely do improve. It is not just the grades that demonstrate to me their improvement; in my writing classes, students complete a self-analysis of their course-work through the class and overwhelmingly they realize themselves the advances they have accomplished in their academic writing.

Writing is such a powerful tool. Everyone should be writing.
~Firoozeh Dumas

You too have become one of my students and we've spent a great deal of time together through this book. You ought to have learned some new editing strategies and hopefully practiced them all through these paragraphs. Now, you know and understand the three reasons for grammar errors and have applied them throughout the book. If you have done all the edits (and I assume you have!), you've become better at editing the verb forms of irregular verbs and verbals. You are now more comfortable identifying and correctly using the verb tense patterns. Also, your subject verb agreement usage should be improved. If you've taken time to look up the new vocabulary from the AWL, then your writing will be better with more academic words. Maybe you have even examined some of the different possibilities for writing academic paragraphs. I hope you have written a response or two for the quotes given in Appendix H. I am sure that you can take all these concepts you have been practicing here and continue to apply them to your own future writing as well.

The time that you have invested in this process will have substantial benefits. Why might this be so?

> ## 👓
> ## *Why should anyone exert such effort for excellence in English writing?*

Writing proficiently and using grammar correctly are powerful tools to convey precise* meaning in written contexts. On paper, an equal opportunity for success truly exists regardless of ethnicity, gender, socioeconomic class, or language background. Moreover in our technology-driven global society, writing well is a prized skill in most environments. As Margaret Atwood stated, "A word after a word after a word is power." I would warrant* that every student who desires and works for it can have the power of language superiority. Much of my own academic and career success has occurred because I spent the time and energy to master the essentials of quality language. I wholeheartedly* believe that if you continue on your journey of English mastery, you too can have superior, even sensational academic texts.

It is a funny thing about life,
if you refuse to accept anything but the best,
you very often get it.
~W. Somerset Maugham

Thanks for Coming!

Writing is hard for everyone, even for me; writing this book has been extremely difficult and has taken me about 18 months. I have sweated and bled to get these words on these pages in this manner. Nonetheless, I am one of the lucky ones in my ability to make a career in a profession that I love. While teaching like any other job has its pros and cons, the enabling of others to become more than they are, to meet their personal goals, and to achieve the unimaginable is worth all the difficulty that comes with the task.

I want to take this opportunity to thank you for coming into my classroom and allowing me to share my strategies and practices for verb form improvement with you. I am so fortunate to be able to impart my knowledge in an effort to facilitate your development! It is my earnest❖ desire that you continue to push yourself and improve your academic writing so that you can meet your personal goals, whatever they may be. I believe you can be a successful English writer. I believe in you!

Study Tip

Academic research suggests it takes language learners seven to ten years to acquire a language at an advanced level. American college is certainly considered advanced. I encourage you to relish❖ your improvements and build on them to continue your betterment❖ of English writing! Don't get discouraged by the amount of time it takes. Just keep on keeping on! And as you can, try and have a bit of fun, for me, OK?

So Long for Now!

I've never liked goodbyes; neither did one of my favorite authors Dr. Seuss, who wrote,

Don't cry because it's over, smile because it happened!

Our journey together for now is done. Did you have a good time? I did. Did you learn anything? I defininitely did! I've greatly enjoyed this experience, yet there is much more to come! This is the first in a series of grammar editing books that will be available for you to purchase and enjoy.

When? Soon.

Remember, writing is hard! And it takes more time than either you or I can even imagine now. Currently residing in my head and slowly working their way down my fingers onto my computer are the *Editing Academic Texts* topics of Verb Tense, Nouns and Articles, Adjectives and Adverbs, Prepositions, Sentence Boundary Problems, Clause Types, Sentence Patterns, and more.

Furthermore, this isn't really goodbye anyway. You can stay in touch with me if you like and keep abreast❖ of what's upcoming by visiting my website at www.clmn.net. You can email me at classroom@clmn.net and let me know what you thought of the book or learned from the strategies or edits. I'd love to hear about how you applied these strategies in your own editing process! Writing improvement is not a solo❖ endeavor; we are a community of learners and writers all working together for the goal of better more effective communication.

"What we learn with pleasure we never forget.
~Alfred Mercier

CHAPTER 10

APPENDICES

The big secret in life is there is no big secret.

Whatever your goal, you can get there

if you're willing to work.

   ~Oprah Winfrey

Appendix A: Abbreviation List and Formula Index

Abbreviations

- Academic Word List – AWL
- Base Form – BF
- English as a Second Language - ESL
- Future – FTR
- Future Participle – FTR PART
- Modal – MDL
- Past – PST
- Past Participle – PST PART
- Present – PRS
- Present Participle – PRS PART

Formulas

(FORMULA INDICATED)

[regular and irregular verb form examples indicated]

- Base Form – (Verb) [edit]
- Present Participle All Verbs – (Verb + ING) [edit]
- Past Form – Regular Verbs (BF + ED) or Irregular Verbs (Varies) *[edited / wrote]*
- Past Participle – Regular Verbs (BF + ED) or Irregular Verbs (Varies) *[edited / written]*
- Active Voice Past Simple - Regular Verbs (BF + ED) or Irregular Verbs(Varies) *[edited / wrote]*
- Active Voice Present Simple - (BF) or (BF + S) *[edit / edits]*
- Active Voice Future Simple- (FTR + BF) *[will edit]*
- Active Voice Past Continuous – (PST BE + PRS PART) *[was / were editing]*
- Active Voice Present Continuous – (PRS BE + PRS PART) *[am / is / are editing]*
- Active Voice Future Continuous – (FTR BE + PRS PART) *[will be editing]*
- Active Voice Past Perfect – (PST HAVE + PST PART) *[had edited]*
- Active Voice Present Perfect (PRS HAVE + PST PART) *[have / has edited]*
- Active Voice Future Perfect (FTR HAVE + PST PART) *[will have edited]*
- Active Voice Past Perfect Continuous – (PST HAVE + PST PART BE + PRS PART) *[had been editing]*
- Active Voice Present Perfect Continuous (PRS HAVE + PST PART BE + PRS PART) *[have / has been editing]*
- Active Voice Future Perfect Continuous (FTR HAVE + PST PART BE + PRS PART) *[will have been editing]*
- Active Voice Modals Simple - (MDL + BF) *[can edit]*
- Active Voice Modals Continuous - (MDL + BE + PRS PART) *[can be editing]*

- Active Voice Modals Perfect - (MDL + HAVE + PST PART) *[can have edited]*
- Active Voice Modals Perfect Continuous - (MDL + HAVE + PST PART BE + PRS PART) *[can have been editing]*
- Passive Voice Past Simple – (PST BE + PST PART) *[was / were editing]*
- Passive Voice Present Simple – (PRS BE + PST PART) *[am / is / are edited]*
- Passive Voice Future Simple – (FTR BE + PST PART) *[will be edited]*
- Passive Voice Past Continuous – (PST BE + PRS PART BE + PST PART) *[was / were being edited]*
- Passive Voice Present Continuous – (PRS BE + PRS PART BE + PST PART) *[am / is / are being edited]*
- Passive Voice Past Perfect – (PST HAVE + PST PART BE + PST PART) *[was / were been edited]*
- Passive Voice Present Perfect – (PRS HAVE + PST PART BE + PST PART) *[have / has been edited]*
- Passive Voice Modals Simple - (MDL + BE + BF) *[can be edited]*
- Passive Voice Modals Continuous - (MDL + BE + PRS PART BE + PST PART) *[can be being edited]*
- Passive Voice Modals Perfect - (MDL + HAVE + PST PART BE + PST PART) *[can have been edited]*

Appendix B: Chart Index

Appendix C: Example Index

Appendix D: Irregular Verb Index

This is not a complete list of every English irregular verb; these are the irregular verbs used in this book.

BASE FORM	PRESENT PART	PAST FORM	PAST PART
arise	arising	arose	arisen
be	being	was/were	been
become	becoming	became	become
begin	beginning	began	begun
break	breaking	broke	broke
build	building	built	built
buy	buying	bought	bought
catch	catching	caught	caught
choose	choosing	chose	chosen
come	coming	came	came
cut	cutting	cut	cut
do	doing	did	done
draw	drawing	drew	drawn
drink	drinking	drank	drunk
drive	driving	drove	driven
fall	falling	fell	fallen
fight	fighting	fought	fought
find	finding	found	found
fling	flinging	flung	flung
feel	feeling	felt	felt
forget	forgetting	forgot	forgotten
freeze	freezing	froze	frozen
get	getting	got	gotten
give	giving	gave	given
grow	growing	grew	grown

BASE FORM	PRESENT PART	PAST FORM	PAST PART
go	going	went	gone
hang	hanging	hung	hung
have	having	had	had
hear	hearing	heard	heard
hit	hitting	hit	hit
hurt	hurting	hurt	hurt
keep	keeping	kept	kept
know	knowing	knew	known
lay	laying	laid	laid
lay out	laying out	laid out	laid out
lead	leading	led	led
leave	leaving	left	left
let	letting	let	let
make	making	made	made
mean	meaning	meant	meant
meet	meeting	met	met
overcome	overcoming	overcame	overcome
overthrow	overthrowing	overthrew	overthrown
pay	paying	paid	paid
put	putting	put	put
read	reading	read	read
ride	writing	wrote	written
rise	rising	rose	risen
run	running	ran	run
say	saying	said	said
see	seeing	saw	send
seek	seeking	sought	sought
send	sending	sent	sent

BASE FORM	PRESENT PART	PAST FORM	PAST PART
sit	sitting	sat	sat
speak	speaking	spoke	spoken
spend	spending	spent	spent
stink	stinking	stank	stunk
swim	swimming	swam	swum
take	taking	took	taken
teach	teaching	taught	taught
tear	tearing	tore	torn
tell	telling	told	told
think	thinking	thought	thought
throw	throwing	threw	thrown
understand	understanding	understood	understood
wear	wearing	wore	worn
write	writing	wrote	written

Appendix E: Works Cited

Allen, Phyllis. "Leaving Identity Issues to Other Folks." *This I Believe: The Personal Philosophies of Remarkable Men and Women.* Edited by Jay Allison, Dan Gediman, John Gregory, and Viki Merrick. Picador, 2007. pp. 10-12.

Asimov, Isaac. "The Fun They Had." *Discovering Fiction 1: A Reader of American Short Stories.* Edited by Judith Jay and Rosemary Gleshenen. Cambridge University Press, 2013. pp. 91-93.

Blanco, Jodee. *Please Stop Laughing at Me.* Adams Media, 2003.

Bradbury, Ray. "Marionettes, Inc." *A Tangled Web.* Edited by Christine Lindop and Alison Sykes-McNulty. Oxford University Press, 2008. pp. 9-18.

Breslaw, Elaine G. Tituba, Reluctant Witch of Salem: Devilish Indians and Puritan Fantasies. University Press, 1996.

Bunn, Mike. "How to Read like a Writer." *Writing Spaces: Readings on Writing Vol 2.* Edited by Charles Lowe and Pavel Zemliansky. Parlor Press, 2010. pp. 71-86.

Clark, Irene L. Writing in the Center: Teaching in a Writing Center Setting. Kendall/Hunt, 1998.

Coleridge, Samuel Taylor. *The Rime of the Ancient Mariner and Other Poems.* Dover Publications, 2012.

Conrad, Joseph. "Heart of Darkness." *The Norton Anthology of British Literature.* Edited by Jon Stallworthy, M.H. Abrams, and Stephen Greenblatt. 7th. Norton & Co, 2003. pp. 1957-2016.

De Beaumont, Madame. *Beauty and the Beast.* Translated by Diane Goode. Bradbury Press, 1978.

Earle, Elizabeth Deutsch. "An Honest Doubter." *This I Believe: The Personal Philosophies of Remarkable Men and Women.* Edited by Jay Allison, Dan Gediman, John Gregory, and Viki Merrick. Picador, 2007. pp. 52-54.

Earle, Elizabeth Deutsch. "Have I Learned Anything Important Since I Was Sixteen?" *This I Believe: The Personal Philosophies of Remarkable Men and Women.* Edited by Jay Allison, Dan Gediman, John Gregory, and Viki Merrick. Picador, 2007. pp. 55-57.

Fauci, Anthony. "A Goal of Service to Mankind." *This I Believe: The Personal Philosophies of Remarkable Men and Women.* Edited by Jay Allison, Dan Gediman, John Gregory, and Viki Merrick. Picador, 2007. pp. 65-67.

Faulkner, William. "Barn Burning." *Collected Stories of William Faulkner.* Random House, 1943. pp. 3-25.

Frost, Robert. "The Road Not Taken." *Poetry Foundation.* Poetry Foundation, 2016. www.poetryfoundation.org/resources/learning/core-poems/detail/44272. Accessed 28 June 2016.

Guild, Pat. "The Culture/Learning Style Connection: Educating for Diversity." *Educational Leadership*, vol. 51, no. 8, 1994. pp. 53-57.

Gup, Ted. "In Praise of the 'Wobblies.'" *This I Believe: The Personal Philosophies of Remarkable Men and Women.* Edited by Jay Allison, Dan Gediman, John Gregory, and Viki Merrick. Picador, 2007. pp. 97-99.

Heinlein, Robert A. "Our Noble, Essential Decency." *This I Believe: The Personal Philosophies of Remarkable Men and Women.* Edited by Jay Allison, Dan Gediman, John Gregory, and Viki Merrick. Picador, 2007. pp. 119-122.

Heinlein, Robert A. Stranger in a Strange Land (Remembering Tomorrow). Ace, 1987.

Henley, William Ernest. "Invictus." *Poetry Foundation.* Poetry Foundation, 2016. www.poetryfoundation.org/poems-and-poets/poems/detail/51642. Accessed 28 June 2016.

Hill, Frances. A Delusion of Satan- The Full Story of the Salem Witch Trials. Doubleday, 1995.

Hine, Thomas. The Rise & Fall of the American Teenager. New York, 1999.

Hinton, Corrine E. "So You've Got a Writing Assignment. Now What?" Writing Spaces: Readings on Writing Vol 1. Edited by Charles Lowe and Pavel Zemliansky. Parlor Press, 2010. pp. 18-33.

Holt, John. "How Teachers Make Children Hate Reading." Responding Voices: A Reader for Emerging Writers. Edited by Jon Ford & Elaine Hughes. McGraw-Hill, 1997.

Hughes, Langston. "Harlem." Poetry Foundation. Poetry Foundation, 2016. https://www.poetryfoundation.org/poems-and-poets/poems/detail/46548 Accessed 28 June 2016.

Hughes, Langston. "Thank You Ma'am." Discovering Fiction 2: A Reader of American Short Stories. Edited by Judith Jay and Rosemary Gleshenen.Cambridge University Press, 2001. pp. 17-19.

Interollo, Lisa. "The Quickening." Discovering Fiction 2: A Reader of American Short Stories. Edited by Judith Jay and Rosemary Gleshenen. Cambridge University Press, 2001. pp. 39-47.

Jackson, Shirley. "The Lottery." Discovering Fiction 2: A Reader of American Short Stories. Edited by Judith Jay and Rosemary Gleshenen. Cambridge University Press, 2001. pp. 93-99.

James, Henry. "Daisy Miller: A Study." *The Norton Anthology of American Literature.* Edited by Nina Baym. 6th ed., Norton & Co, 2003. pp. 468-506.

Jamison, Kay Redfield. "The Benefits of Restlessness and Jagged Edges." *This I Believe: The Personal Philosophies of Remarkable Men and Women.* Edited by Jay Allison, Dan Gediman, John Gregory, and Viki Merrick. Picador, 2007. pp. 126-128.

Johnston, C., and Withers, C. *The Old-Time Schools and Schoolbooks.* Dover Publications, 1963.

Kein, Will. "A Not-So-Random Act of Kindness." *Chicken Soup for the College Soul: 101 Inspirational, Supportive, and Humorous Stories about Life in College.* Edited by Jack Canfield, Mark Victor Hansen, Kimberly Kirberger, Dan Clark. Health Communications, 1999. pp. 188-190.

Mardikian, George. "Why I Close My Restaurant." *This I Believe: The Personal Philosophies of Remarkable Men and Women.* Edited by Jay Allison, Dan Gediman, John Gregory, and Viki Merrick. Picador, 2007. pp. 153-155.

Mehrabian, Albert. Silent Messages: Implicit Communication of Emotions and Attitudes. Wadsworth Publication, 1981.

Miller, Arthur, and Weales, Gerald Clifford. *Death of a Salesman.* Penguin, 1996.

Miles, Jamie. "Experiment." *Chicken Soup for the Soul Campus Chronicles: 101 Inspirational, Supportive, and Humorous Stories about Life in College.* Edited by Jack Canfield, Mark Victor Hansen, Amy Newmark, and Madeline Clapps. Chicken Soup for the Soul Publishing, 2009. pp. 44-46.

Oher, Michael and Yaeger, Don. I Beat the Odds: from Homelessness, to The Blind Side, and Beyond. Gotham, 2012.

O. Henry. "The Last Leaf." *Discovering Fiction 2: A Reader of American Short Stories.* Edited by Judith Jay and Rosemary Gleshenen. Cambridge University Press, 2001. pp. 66-70

Patel, Eboo. "We Are Each Other's Business." *This I Believe: The Personal Philosophies of Remarkable Men and Women.* Edited by Jay Allison, Dan Gediman, John Gregory, and Viki Merrick. Picador, 2007. pp. 178-180.

Perkins, David. "The Ancient Mariner and its Interpreters: Some Versions of Coleridge". *Modern Language Quarterly.* Vol. 57 no. 3, Sept 1996.

Perrault, Charles. "Bluebeard". *Classic French Fairy Tales.* Meredith Press, 1967. pp. 39-51.

Pink, Daniel. H. "Chapter 1: The Rise and Fall of Motivation 2.0." *Drive: the Surprising Truth about What Motivates Us.* Riverhead , 2012. pp. 9-20.

Porter, Steve. "The 50-Percent Theory of Life." *This I Believe: The Personal Philosophies of Remarkable Men and Women.* Edited by Jay Allison, Dan Gediman, John Gregory, and Viki Merrick. Picador,2007. pp. 181-183.

Powell, Colin. "The America I Believe In." *This I Believe: The Personal Philosophies of Remarkable Men and Women.* Edited by Jay Allison, Dan Gediman, John Gregory, and Viki Merrick. Picador, 2007. pp. 184-187.

Reid, Shelly. "Ten Ways to Think about Writing: Metaphoric Musings for College Writing." *Writing Spaces: Readings on Writing Vol 2.* Edited by Charles Lowe and Pavel Zemliansky. Parlor Press, 2010. pp. 71-86.

Reid, Joy. M. *Teaching ESL Writing.* Prentice Hall Regents, 1993.

Rittenberg, Josh. "Tomorrow Will Be a Better Day." *This I Believe: The Personal Philosophies of Remarkable Men and Women.* Edited by Jay Allison, Dan Gediman, John Gregory, and Viki Merrick. Picador, 2007. pp.194-196.

Quick, Amanda. *Seduction.* Bantam, 1990.

---. . *Rendezvous.* Bantam, 1991.

---. *Mystique.* Bantam, 1994.

Shoemaker, E.C. Noah Webster: Pioneer of learning. AMS Press, 1966.

Stewart-Copier, Cynthia. "If the Dream Is Big Enough, The Facts Don't Fit." *Chicken Soup for the College Soul:101 Inspirational, Supportive, and Humorous Stories about Life in College.* Edited by Jack Canfield, Mark Victor Hansen, Kimberly Kirberger, Dan Clark. Health Communications, 1999. pp. 20-22.

Twain, M. "Adventures of Huckleberry Finn." *The Norton Anthology of American Literature.* Edited by Nina Baym. 6th ed. Norton & Co, 2003. pp. 219-407.

Tompson, JeVon. "Second Kind of Mind." *Chicken Soup for the College Soul: 101 Inspirational, Supportive, and Humorous Stories about Life in College.* Edit by Jack Canfield, Mark Victor Hansen, Kimberly Kirberger, Dan Clark. Health Communications, 1999. pp. 263-265.

Torcasino, Rosa. "Never Say Never." *Chicken Soup for the College Soul:101 Inspirational, Supportive, and Humorous Stories about Life in College.* Edited by Jack Canfield, Mark Victor Hansen, Kimberly Kirberger, Dan Clark. Health Communications, 1999. pp. 6-8.

Wade, Lisa. "Ten Things Every College Professor Hates." *Business Insider.* August 26, 2016. http://www.businessinsider.com/10-things-every-college-professor-hates-2014-8. Accessed 28 June 2016.

Walker, Alice. *The Color Purple.* Simon & Schuster, 1982.

Warfel, H.R. Noah Webster: Schoolmaster to America. Macmillan Co, 1936.

Warren, Robert Penn. "A Poem of Pure Imagination: An Experiment in Reading". *Twentieth Century Interpretations of The Rime of the Ancient Mariner.* Edited by James D Boulger. Prentice Hall, 1969. pp. 21-47.

Wright, Walter F. *Romance and Tragedy in Joseph Conrad.* University of Nebraska Press, 1949.

Appendix F: Paragraph Information

While any text can be used to practice one's editing skills, narrowing the practice on the target type of material can be extremely effective. For that reason, the Practice Edit paragraphs themselves are related to the kinds of writing you might find in a college class. All of the paragraphs have been written by me; some are from assignments in classes I've taken myself, some are from examples in classes I've taught, and some were written just for this book. Although this is not intended to be a composition instruction guide, the paragraphs are generally written following good writing content and rules as taught in my own writing courses, so may be used as exemplary model writing as well. The Paragraph Types explains each kind of paragraph used and lists the examples while the Paragraph Topics defines the kinds of content used and lists the examples of each. Also included here is a chart with each edit number, paragraph, paragraph type, paragraph topic, and page number for easy reference.

Please note that in these definitions, the author is the creator of a published text, as in CC Undertree is the author of this book, whereas the writer is the creator of an unpublished paper about the text, as in you are the writer of your own paper.

Paragraph Types

- **Essay Paragraph** - This kind of paragraph should have a main idea, either explicit or implicit, with examples and explanation to prove the main idea. Examples of essay paragraphs can be seen in the Practice Edits: 2, 6, 7, 8, 11, 16, 17, 19, 20, 21, 22, 23, 24, 26, 27, 28, 29, 30, 31, 32, 33, 34, 35.

- **Summary** - This kind of paragraph succinctly states the main ideas of an author's written work, but uses the writer's own vocabulary and sentence structure; it does not consider the writer's opinion, but rather reports the author's ideas only, using primarily only third person point of view. Examples of summary paragraphs can be seen in the Practice Edits: 3, 14, 15, 36, 37, 38, 39, 40, & 43.

- **Response** - In this kind of paragraph, the writer selects an idea or ideas from an author's written work and applies these concepts to his or her own personal experiences. Many blogs follow this general format. First person point of view is primarily used. Examples of response paragraphs can be seen in the Practice Edits: 1, 12, 4, 24, 41, & 42.

- **Summary Response** - This kind of paragraph provides a summary of one or two of the ideas from an author's written work as in the summary described above and then responds to these ideas with a personal application to the writer's own ideas as in the response described above. Examples of summary response paragraphs can be seen in the Practice Edits: 5, 9, 10, 13, 18, 25, 44, 45, 46, 47, 50, 51,& 53.

- **Academic Articles** - Academic Articles are used as texts in many college classes including English writing, general education, and specific major courses. These texts are written at the college level or higher and follow standard argumentative format by making a claim and providing evidence to prove it. These kinds of texts often come from journals, books, or websites. Examples of academic article paragraphs can be seen in the Practice Edits: 1, 7, 8, 12, 16, 17, 19, 20, 21, 22, 23, 24, 29, 30, 40, 41, 43, & 44.

- **Poems and Plays**- Poems are used as text mostly in English writing and literature classes though they may be used to enhance the academic articles in any college class. They are a literary work using specific structures including meter, rhyme and stanza. Because poems are shorter than other works, they are often published in anthologies though many websites provide individual poems as well. Plays are generally only read in English Literature classes and are the script of the plot and language that is acted out on the stage. Examples of poem or play paragraphs can be seen in the Practice Edits: 2, 4, 28, 42, & 45.

- **Fiction Novels and Short Stories**- Fiction Novels are used as creative texts mostly in English writing and literature classes though they may be used to enhance the academic articles in any college class. Short Stories follow the same general aspects of the longer novel, in that imaginary events and people are described in a story format, but short stories are shorter in length with a condensed story. Novels are stand-alone works, but short stories are often published in anthologies though many websites provide individual short stories as well. Examples of fiction novel and short story paragraphs can be seen in the Practice Edits:6, 11, 14, 15, 26, 27, 31, 32, 33, 34, 35, 36, 37, 46,

- **Nonfiction Narratives**- Nonfiction Narratives, also called Memoirs, are used as creative texts mostly in English writing and literature classes though they may be used to enhance the academic articles in any college class. These kinds of text employ some of the structures of fiction like character development and plot, but unlike fiction, nonfiction narratives are based on true events or circumstances in the author's life. Moreover, they can be produced in a stand-alone length much like a novel or in an anthology in short-story length. Many of today's blogs are a type of nonfiction narrative. Examples of nonfiction narrative paragraphs can be seen in the Practice Edits:3, 5, 9, 10, 13, 18, 25, 38, 39, 47, 48, 49, 50, 51, 52, & 53.

EDIT #	TYPE	TOPIC	CH	PG #
Edit 1	Response	Academic Article	3	41
Edit 2	Essay Paragraph	Poem	3	43
Edit 3	Summary	Nonfiction Narrative	3	45
Edit 4	Response	Poem	3	47
Edit 5	Summary Response	Nonfiction Narrative	3	49
Edit 6	Essay Paragraph	Fiction Short Story	4	59
Edit 7	Essay Paragraph	Academic Article	4	61
Edit 8	Essay Paragraph	Academic Article	4	63
Edit 9	Summary Response	Nonfiction Narrative	4	65
Edit 10	Summary Response	Nonfiction Narrative	4	67
Edit 11	Essay Paragraph	Fiction Novel	5	85
Edit 12	Response	Academic Article	5	87
Edit 13	Summary Response	Nonfiction Narrative	5	89
Edit 14	Summary	Fiction Short Story	5	91
Edit 15	Summary	Fiction Short Story	5	93
Edit 16	Essay Paragraph	Academic Article	6	109
Edit 17	Essay Paragraph	Academic Article	6	111
Edit 18	Summary Response	Nonfiction Narrative	6	113
Edit 19	Essay Paragraph	Academic Article	6	115
Edit 20	Essay Paragraph	Academic Article	6	117
Edit 21	Essay Paragraph	Academic Article	7	125
Edit 22	Essay Paragraph	Academic Article	7	127
Edit 23	Essay Paragraph	Academic Article	7	129
Edit 24	Essay Paragraph	Academic Article	7	131
Edit 25	Summary Response	Nonfiction Narrative	7	133
Edit 26	Essay Paragraph	Fiction Novel	8	139
Edit 27	Essay Paragraph	Fiction Novel	8	141
Edit 28	Essay Paragraph	Play	8	143

EDIT #	TYPE	TOPIC	CH	PG #
Edit 29	Essay Paragraph	Academic Article	8	145
Edit 30	Essay Paragraph	Academic Article	8	147
Edit 31	Essay Paragraph	Fiction Short Story	8	149
Edit 32	Essay Paragraph	Fiction Short Story	8	151
Edit 33	Essay Paragraph	Fiction Short Story	8	153
Edit 34	Essay Paragraph	Fiction Short Story	8	155
Edit 35	Essay Paragraph	Fiction Short Story	8	157
Edit 36	Summary	Fiction Short Story	8	159
Edit 37	Summary	Fiction Short Story	8	161
Edit 38	Summary	Nonfiction Narrative	8	163
Edit 39	Summary	Nonfiction Narrative	8	165
Edit 40	Summary	Academic Article	8	167
Edit 41	Response	Academic Article	8	169
Edit 42	Response	Poem	8	171
Edit 43	Summary	Academic Article	8	173
Edit 44	Summary Response	Academic Article	8	175
Edit 45	Summary Response	Poem	8	177
Edit 46	Summary Response	Fictional Short Story	8	179
Edit 47	Summary Response	Nonfiction Narrative	8	181
Edit 48	Summary	Nonfiction Narrative	8	183
Edit 49	Summary	Nonfiction Narrative	8	185
Edit 50	Summary Response	Nonfiction Narrative	8	187
Edit 51	Summary Response	Nonfiction Narrative	8	189
Edit 52	Summary Response	Nonfiction Narrative	8	191
Edit 53	Summary Response	Nonfiction Narrative	8	193

Appendix G: Quote Index

In my writing classes, I'm a big proponent of free writing to increase the flow of language and words on the paper. I often use motivating or thought-provoking quotes from others to start out a writing session. If you'd like to practice your own free writing too, here are the quotes used in the book. In responding to these ideas, you can ask yourself:

- How does this idea apply to my own experience?
- Do I have an example in my life that I can relate to this quote?
- How do I feel about this idea?
- Do I agree or disagree with this idea? Why?
- Would embracing this idea make me a better writer? Student? Human being?
- How does this quote apply to other concepts I've learned? Books I've read? Movies I've seen?

Try writing a paragraph response to one or more of these quotes. You could use the summary response paragraphs throughout the book as models for academic format. When you're finished, make sure to double check those verb forms!

1. Only those who dare to fail greatly can ever achieve greatly. ~ Robert Kennedy
2. One today is worth two tomorrows; never leave for tomorrow what you can do today. ~ Benjamin Franklin
3. Knowing what you want is the first step to getting it. ~ Louise Hart
4. Live as if you were to die tomorrow. Learn as if you were to live forever. ~ Mahatma Gandhi
5. The beautiful thing about learning is that nobody can take it away from you. ~ B.B. King
6. Education is the passport to the future, for tomorrow belongs to those who prepare for it today. ~ Malcolm X
7. Champions keep playing until they get it right. ~ Billy Jean King
8. O someone should start laughing! Someone should start widely Laughing Now! ~ Hafez
9. Nothing great was ever achieved without enthusiasm. ~ Ralph Waldo Emerson
10. It isn't where you come from; it's where you are going that counts. ~ Ella Fitzgerald
11. If you think you can, you're right. And if you think you can't, you're right. ~ Mary Kay Ash
12. If we did all the things we are capable of doing, we would literally astound ourselves. ~ Thomas Edison
13. Writing is the hardest work in the world not involving heavy lifting. ~ Pete Hamill
14. I didn't get here dreaming about it or thinking about it. I got here by doing it. ~ Estee Lauder
15. Decide what you want, decide what you are willing to exchange for it. Establish your priorities and go to work. ~ H. L. Hunt
16. What really matters is what you do with what you have. ~ Shirley Lord
17. Success isn't measured by the position you reach in life; it's measured by the obstacles you overcome. ~ Booker T. Washington

18. Success is no accident. It is hard work, perseverance, learning, studying, sacrifice and most of all, love of what you are doing or learning to do. ~ Pele

19. If you don't like something, change it; if you can't change it, change the way you think about it. ~ Mary Engelbreit

20. Failure is the opportunity to begin again more intelligently. ~ Henry Ford

21. You can't try to do things; you simply must do them. ~ Ray Bradbury

22. Mistakes are portals of discovery. ~ James Joyce

23. Knock the "t" off the "can't." ~ George Reeves

24. Little by little does the trick. ~ Aesop

25. One always has enough time, if one will apply it well. ~ Johann Wolfgang von Goethe

26. We become what we do. ~ Chiang Kai-Shek

27. Failure is a success if we learn from it. ~ Malcolm Forbes

28. The truth of the matter is that you always know the right thing to do. The hard part is doing it.
    ~ H. Norman Schwarzkopf

29. There is nothing to writing. All you do is sit down at a typewriter and bleed. ~ Ernest Hemingway

30. Writing is such a powerful tool. Everyone should be writing. ~ Firoozeh Dumas

31. A word after a word after a word is power. ~ Margaret Atwood

32. It is a funny thing about life, if you refuse to accept anything but the best, you very often get it.
    ~ W. Somerset Maugham

33. "Don't cry because it's over, smile because it happened." ~ Dr. Seuss

34. "What we learn with pleasure we never forget. ~ Alfred Mercier

35. The big secret in life is that there is no big secret. Whatever your goal, you can get there if you're willing to work.
    ~ Oprah Winfrey

36. A dream doesn't become reality through magic; it takes sweat, determination, and hard work. ~ Colin Powel

Appendix H: Vocabulary Index

Oftentimes when ESL students are reading college texts, they can become overwhelmed by the sheer number of unknown words. Looking up every single unknown word is not the most effective strategy in most cases. There are many techniques for identifying which vocabulary words need to be given extra time; here, the focus is on the vocabulary from the Academic World List. If while reading the text, you didn't know any of the words indicated with the *, you should take the time to learn them as they are all basic English vocabulary that should be comprehended and used at a college level. If you truly want to challenge yourself, review some of the included bonus vocabulary indicated throughout with a ✦.

Using the AWL effectively will take time, but it can greatly improve your vocabulary. Here you will find a compilation of the words used in the book from the AWL list and the page number where each can be found. If you see that you aren't familiar with one of these words, you can look it up in a good English dictionary. My personal favorite is *Merriam-Webster Collegiate Dictionary*; a great ESL specific one is *Merriam-Webster Learner's Dictionary*. As you study these words, you can note how each word is used in the original sentence as the page number next to each tells you where you can find it in this book. Also, identify any other related word forms. Practice using this vocabulary in your own work! It's that easy to expand your language usage!

AWL Vocabulary indicated with a * throughout

Front Matter pp i-x

grant	ii	item	iii	edit	viii	final	ix
purchase	ii	panel	viii	colleague	ix	appreciate	ix
transmit	ii						

Chapter 1: Introduction pp 1-14

instructor	3	method	4	design	5	survey	7
technique	3	incorporate	4	paragraph	5	shift	7
required	3	prior	4	aspect	6	indicate	7
complex	3	enable	4	error	6	aid	7
target	3	concept	4	area	6	crucial	8
available	3	context	5	specific	6	circumstance	8
focus	3	relevant	5	benefit	6	create	8
secure	4	comprehensive	5	strategy	6	indicate	8
structure	4	scope	5	participle	7	conclude	8
primary	4	resource	5	indefinite	7	summary	8
reinforces	4	assume	5	isolate	7	cite	8

Bonus Vocabulary Not on the AWL indicated with a ❖throughout

grassroots	viiii	grueling	15	ideology	50	facetiously	197
spur	viiii	genre	16	loath	50	arduous	197
embolden	viiii	resounding	16	mimic	82	equivalently	197
recompense	ix	exasperate	16	invert	83	momentous	197
camaraderie	ix	rectify	16	onerous	88	warrant	198
unflagging	ix	discern	18	obligatory	97	precise	198
galvanize	ix	sheer	18	unceasingly	99	wholeheartedly	198
angst	ix	interminable	19	mitigate	101	relish	199
wisecrack	ix	zero-in	21	imperative	107	earnest	199
encompass	3	compel	26	elucidate	114	betterment	199
multi-faceted	3	vehement	29	mock	118	abreast	200
scholastic	3	baffling	31	erroneous	121	solo	200
strive	3	dispute	31	prohibit	121	engender	224
herein	4	ascertain	31	boost	121	intricacy	224
coalesce	7	gratify	32	belie	126	inclusion	224
accentuate	9	nitty-gritty	32	muse	144		
shambles	10	atypical	38	yearn	152		
simultaneous	10	mythic	44	minutia	184		

Appendix I: Fun Suggestions

Having fun with tedious tasks can certainly be a challenge. You are probably much more creative than I about things that you enjoy and give you pleasure. You can brainstorm your own ideas for having fun too. Here are some ways to have fun with editing that I've come up with. Try one of these or write your own!

1. Pay yourself for every error you find and correct.
2. Buy some happy stickers and put one on your paper once you've completed a final edit.
3. Get some awesome colored pens that are fun to write with (I like purple!) and only use them for editing.
4. Reward yourself for a good edit with your favorite snack or candy. Chocolate is always a reward!
5. Download a time tracking app and track the actual time you spend editing. Be amazed at how much time it takes!
6. Have an editing party with some friends. Whoever finds the most mistakes gets to choose the movie!
7. Do something fun for yourself once you've spent the required time like go to the beach in Southern California or the park somewhere else.
8. Create an editing music mix of your favorite study songs to edit by. Only use it during your editing.
9. Share your secrets of success with all your friends and watch them be awed by your greatness.
10. Read your favorite book or watch a TV show you like as a reward for a job well done.

Write your own suggestions below!

11.

12.

13.

14.

15. Have some fun!

A dream doesn't become reality through magic; it takes sweat, determination, and hard work.

~Colin Powel

About the Author

CC Undertree, a pseudonym for Catherine Coleman, is a language and English writing instructor in Southern California, USA. With an M.A. in Linguistics, B.A. in English, Post-Graduate Certificate in Teaching English as a Second Language, and a Post-Graduate Certificate in Reading Instruction, she has been helping students master the intricacies* of English reading, writing, speaking and listening since she began as a college peer tutor in 1999. Having taught in a variety of settings including private language schools, state college, university, and community colleges, she has been privileged to teach writing and editing techniques to a diverse student population.

In addition to her classroom teaching, Prof. Undertree also maintains Coleman's Classroom, a platform to engage, educate, and empower. On her website at www.ccundertree.com, she provides an assortment of educational materials. Most recently, she has branched into the world of digital education with her CC Undertree channel on Youtube. You can also find her on Instagram @ ccundertree or Facebook @ CiCiUndertree.

Prof. Undertree has several goals for all her educational materials and lessons. The first is to provide a place of inclusion* for all learners where everyone is welcome. Another is to provide quality, pragmatic information to facilitate students' language development. A bonus would be to engender* a passion for the power of good English and the possibility of excellence. Her ultimate goal is to teach herself out of a job, for when the instructor has become redundant because the student has become his or her own instructor, Prof. Undertree will have achieved her supreme success. She aims high, no less than changing the world – one word, one story, one student at a time.

CPSIA information can be obtained
at www.ICGtesting.com
Printed in the USA
LVHW062319100919
630677LV00011B/155/P